"Quilting News of Yesteryear"

Schiffer Publishing Ltd

4880 Lower Valley Road, Atglen, PA 19310 USA

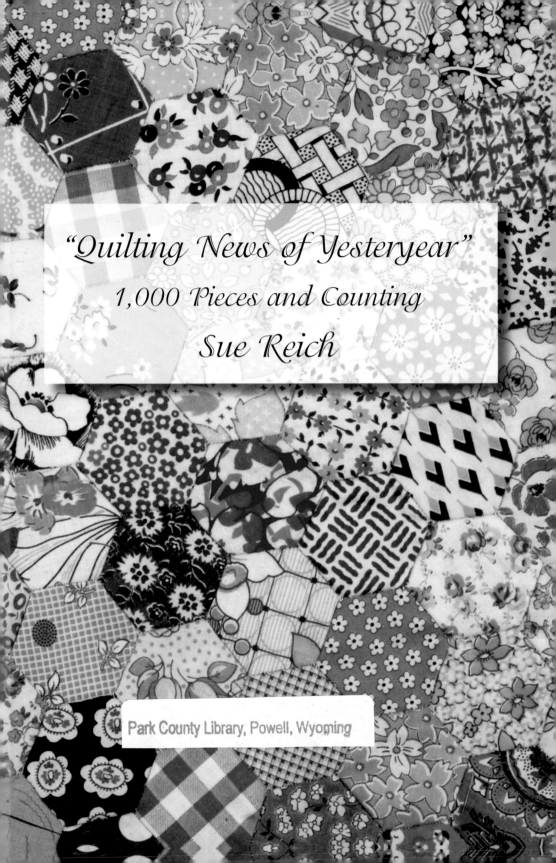

"Quilting News of Yesteryear"

1,000 Pieces and Counting

Sue Reich

Published by Schiffer Publishing Ltd.
4880 Lower Valley Road
Atglen, PA 19310
Phone: (610) 593-1777; Fax: (610) 593-2002
E-mail: Info@schifferbooks.com

For the largest selection of fine reference books on this and related subjects, please visit
our web site at www.schifferbooks.com
We are always looking for people to write books on new and related subjects. If you have
an idea for a book please contact us at the above address.

This book may be purchased from the publisher.
Include $3.95 for shipping.
Please try your bookstore first.
You may write for a free catalog.

In Europe, Schiffer books are distributed by
Bushwood Books
6 Marksbury Ave.
Kew Gardens
Surrey TW9 4JF England
Phone: 44 (0) 20 8392-8585; Fax: 44 (0) 20 8392-9876
E-mail: info@bushwoodbooks.co.uk
Website: www.bushwoodbooks.co.uk

Library of Congress Control Number: 2006931698

Layout by John P. Cheek
Cover design by Bruce Waters
Type set in Isadora/New Basketville BT
ISBN: 0-7643-2595-7
Printed in China

Dedication

**Major Stephen Reich
killed in action
Afghanistan
June 28, 2005
Your love and devotion
to your family, men and country
is what sustains me, and
encourages me to go on.**

Introduction

Quilts made with thousands of pieces of fabric are seen at quilt documentation days, presented at quilt appraisal tables, and are archived in museums and historical societies. They range from predictable crazy quilts, in which irregularly shaped scraps, left over from dress and hat making projects, were applied to a foundation base and fancied up with decorative embroidery work, to the precisely cut, identical shapes pieced in charm quilts, whose magic appeal was in the variety of the prints. We know what quilts with *multitudinous pieces* look like. The question that frequently arises is "Why did quiltmakers save, piece, and then quilt those itsy-bitsy scraps of fabrics into bed-sized objects of the decorative arts?"

In 2000, while researching for "*Quilts and Quiltmakers Covering Connecticut,*" the documentation book of the Connecticut Quilt Search Project, I discovered the following newspaper clipping in the archives of the Willimantic Chronicle dated November 29, 1882, Columbia:

> "In the last issue of the Chronicle we noticed a lady in South Coventry has completed a bed quilt consisting of 6,360 pieces and was consequently victor – we are informed Miss Sophia C. Yeomans has recently pieced an elegant silk quilt consisting of 7,524 pieces exceeding the above mentioned by 1,164 pieces. When that is beaten we will try again."

I found surprising the newsprint's reference to making quilts with thousands pieces as a *competition*! In later archives of the Willimantic Chronicle, there were ongoing accounts of Connecticut maidens and matrons meeting the challenge to outdo and out piece one another with even greater numbers of scraps per quilt.

1,000 Pieces and Counting is the first book in a series of "*Quilting News of Yesteryear.*" It features over 300 newsprint items spanning one hundred years. As you read these accounts, you will see the emergence of other fads in quiltmaking such as charm quilts and crazy quilts. They are reported historically along with other *multitudinous-pieced* quilts. Our country's Centennial celebration seems to be pivotal to these new fads in quiltmaking. The competitive aspect of creating quilts with thousands of pieces became a nationwide obsession beginning shortly before 1876. The propensity for quiltmakers to piece in behemoth numbers in contest with one another increases sharply during the 1880s. Crazy quilts and charm quilts were shorter-lived fads within this fascination for making quilts with thousands of pieces. Newsprint reports of quilts of *multitudinous-pieces* continues well into the twentieth century but in fewer numbers.

Quiltmakers of the third and fourth quarter of the nineteenth century were the original fabric hounds. Using a variety of fabrics and patterns, quiltmakers showed off the abundance in their textile collections. The quantities and diversity of fabrics in their quilts illustrate some degree of economic prosperity in the greater society-at-large. Many of these quilts were made in a one-patch design. The simple square set straight or on point, was the most popular. Other popular one-patch quilts made with thousands of pieces; include hexagons, rectangles, triangles, diamonds, oblongs, tumblers, clam shells and herringbones. Patterned quilts with more varied blocks were less commonly made in the thousands of pieces, and crazy quilts were reported as a subcategory within this trend.

Quilt history researchers spend years seeking out journals, diaries, quiltmaking notes, templates, and similar materials, to explain and validate our notions for the inspiration, the techniques, and the artistic inclination of ancestral quiltmakers. Without primary source records, we often superimpose our twenty-first century views of quiltmaking on the anonymous quilters of centuries past. Now with the advancement of technology, there are more and more sophisticated methods of conducting this research. Today, searchable, online newspapers bring journalistic reports of the quiltmaking of yesteryear to our fingertips. Now, researchers can utilize a new perspective in our study of women and their quiltmaking history.

1,000 Pieces and Counting presents two collections combining secondary source data, and quilted examples of the styles indicated in the news articles. When possible, I have chosen quilts contemporary in time to the newsprint in order to provide a visual connection for the reader. From a distance, *multitudinous-pieced* quilts usually don't have much visual appeal unless the quiltmaker organized her pieces into a particular color scheme. The fascination with this genre of quilts is in the massive collections of fabrics in one textile. The quilts you will find here range in number of pieces from approximately 750 to 8,500. It is very hard to comprehend a quilt with pieces that number in five digits. Yet, Memorial Hall Museum in Deerfield, Massachusetts, always has on view a diamond quilt top made by a Vermont lady with 82,000 pieces. The diamonds are so small that their width equals the width of the selvage. It is no wonder this quilt was never finished. The prospect of needling through five layers would discourage any quiltmaker!

I would like to take this opportunity to thank the staff at Schiffer Publications, Ltd., for their co-operation and encouragement in this project. Also, a special thanks is extended to readers Bonnie Dwyer, Susan Fiondella, and Maureen Gregoire, to Barbara Garrett for her assistance during the photography and to very generous friends who have shared their quilts for the photography of this book.

It is my sincere hope that readers will use the information compiled from newsprints of yesteryear in current research, lectures, and writings. Most of these reports focus only on the amazing numbers of pieces in the quilts. Hopefully, some of these quilts remain in their same communities or can be found housed in historical societies and museums. As the newsprints are out of copyright, the articles have been scrupulously reproduced just as they appeared in print, replete with spelling, punctuation and grammatical mistakes.

The quilts featured in *1,000 Pieces and Counting* begin and end with mosaic paper-pieced patterns that span one hundred years of quiltmaking. These quilts exemplify a timeless piecing technique and continue to be popular even with the quilters of today.

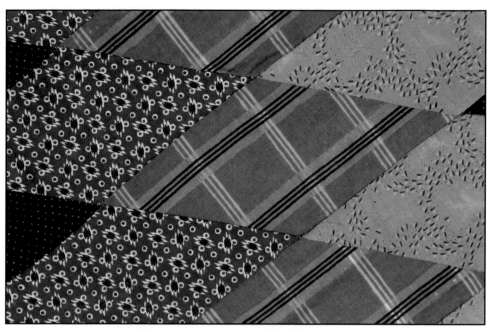

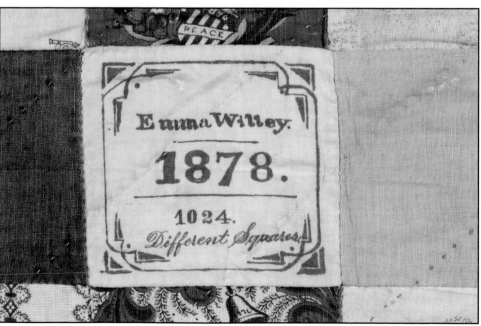

Emma Willey.

1878.

1024.
Different Squares.

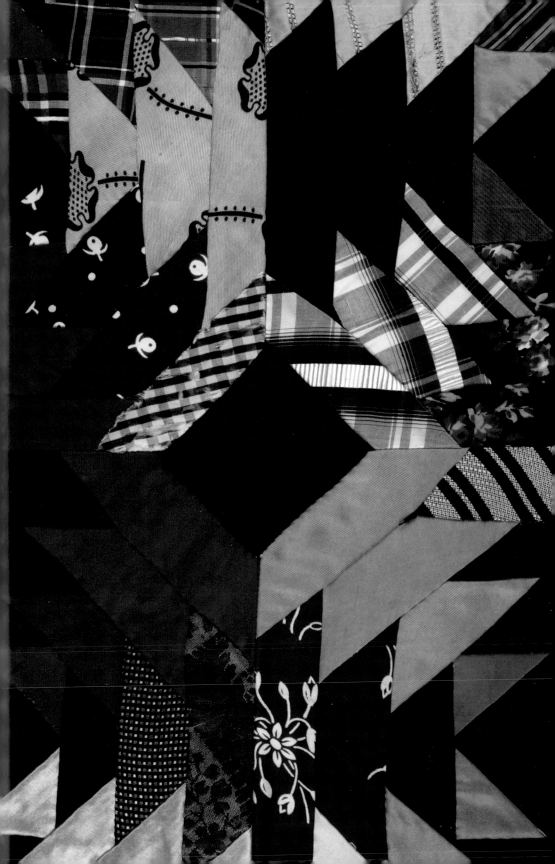

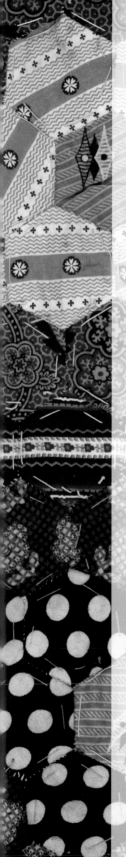

Adams Sentinel
Gettysburg, Pennsylvania
May 12, 1834

Penelope Outdone. —— A young lady in Charleston, S.C. has recently manifested the possession of an uncommon stock of patience and perseverance, in the completion of two great achievements of the needle – a Hexagon Quilt, composed of 7630 pieces, and a Star Quilt composed of 7239 pieces.

Adams Sentinel
Gettysburg, Pennsylvania
November 28, 1836

Quilts. – A lady in this vicinity, has made a quilt containing 2777 pieces. — She will, no doubt, be comfortable when the cold noth-westers visit her this winter. We would say, that she is not only a patient, but a very *piece*-able lady.
Salt River Journal.

Alton Telegraph and Democrat Review
Alton, Illinois
October 26, 1849
and
Defiance Democrat
Defiance, Ohio
January 12, 1850

A Rare Quilt.—One of the most elegant productions that fell under our observation in the hall appropriate for the handiwork of the ladies at our late fair, was a quilt, wrought by Mrs. Charles Taylor, Chicago. It was composed of 9,800 pieces of silk, each of which was about an inch square, and all sewed with exceeding beauty and neatness. Its chief charm, however, was the

great skill evinced in the ingenious blending of colors, as to produce a proper effect in the representation of various figures which ornamented it in every part. A brilliant sun shone in the centre, the moon and stars beamed out from one corner, while in another appeared a storm in the heavens, with lowering clouds and flashes of lightening. Around the border were various designs illustrative of the seasons and of the rapid growth of our Western country. At one place appeared a barren heath, with the Indians and hunters roaming over it; next a trading post, as the first entrance of civilization; next, a military station, with the glorious banner of our country streaming from the flag-staff, then a city, and steamboats and vessels gliding in and out of port. All these, and many other figures which we do not now remember were brought out by the shades of silk used; and in our opinion, the *tout ensemble* was fully equal, if not superior to any thing else upon the ground. It undoubtedly cost an infinite deal of labor, and is well worthy of going down to successive generations as a specimen of the taste evinced by its fair contriver, both as to design and workmanship. We are proud of any daughter of Michigan who is competent to the production of such a work. Who will equal her by a like effort at the next State fair? ——*Detroit Adv.*

Bangor Daily Whig & Courier
Bangor, Maine
June 23, 1855
ONE "OF THE OLDEN TIME" A lady of Plainfield, Mass., aged 80 years, has the past winter,

Front and back close-ups of this c. 1830 quilt top reveal the exquisite attention the quiltmaker paid to fussy cutting (a contemporary term) the patches for her quilt.

MOSAIC, quilt top, c.1830, cotton, 78 x 93 inches, approximately 7,000 pieces.
The stripes in this paper-pieced, mosaic quilt top form diamonds and straight lines
are really pieced mosaic patches aligned to produce an overall lacy effect. This quilt
is in the collection of Ellie Greco, Forked River, New Jersey.

made with her own hands, 17 quilts, consisting of 4300 pieces cut by pattern, worked 978 scallops, cut and made 8 dresses, knit 3 pairs of striped mittens, made butter from two cows, besides the general housework for a family. She has also written over nearly a quare of paper.

Gettysburg Compiler
Gettysburg, Pennsylvania
August 8, 1859

Old Folks' Quilting. – An old folks' quilting took place at Smith Sutton, Mass., a few days since. The "quilting" was done at the house of widow Joshua Lackey, and was attended by sixteen ladies, whose united ages amount to ten hundred and fifty four years. The oldest, Mrs. Joshua Hicks, is 83 years of age, and the youngest, Mrs. Amos Bardon, is 50. Three are upwards of 80; four between 70 and 80; six between 60 and 70; three between 50 and 60. They quilted a quilt of nearly two thousand pieces, put together by Mrs. Lackey, who is upwards of 80 years of age.

The Berkshire County Eagle
Pittsfield, Massachusetts
October 8, 1863

Miss Ellen S. Purchase, Pittsfield, quilt made by a *Miss* of 12 years, (who is a faithful picker up of unconsidered trifles, as this has 2226 pieces, tastefully arranged and neatly sewed,) 50 cents.

Defiance Democrat
Defiance, Ohio
May 12, 1866

This afternoon (Saturday) can be seen at

The Baptist Church a Silk Quilt, prepared by
Mrs. Cole, Mrs. Meyers and the other ladies of
that Church, to aid in procuring a bell. The
exhibition is of course free to all and is pre-
paratory to sending it East for sale.

It is a magnificent piece of needlework, re-
quiring millions of stitches, and what is more,
range-
ment and ornamentation of its various parts.
It is a model of womanly skill and patience
which we trust may be handsomely rewarded
in bringing a good price. The contributions
are in the names of the Sabbath School Schol-
ars of that Church, but the workmanship is
not that of children—far from it. Call and
see it.

Grand Traverse Herald
Traverse City, Michigan
October 22, 1868
Report of the Second Annual Fair of
the Benzie County Agricultural So-
ciety.
Best
Quilt Centre, 3096 pieces, Bessie S.
Holbrook.

Hornellsville Tribune
Hornellsville, New York
August 11, 1869
Mrs. Mary Babcock, of Andover, has a
quilt made up of 3,562 pieces.

Close-ups of the quilt show the striped cotton backing and the woven tape binding in tan, brown and blue. The name of the quilt-maker is inked in the center block of the quilt.

TRIP AROUND THE WORLD, c.1840, cotton, 114 x 114 inches, 3,229 pieces. Signed *"Ann T. Thomas."* This quilt is in the collection of Sue Reich, Washington Depot, Connecticut.

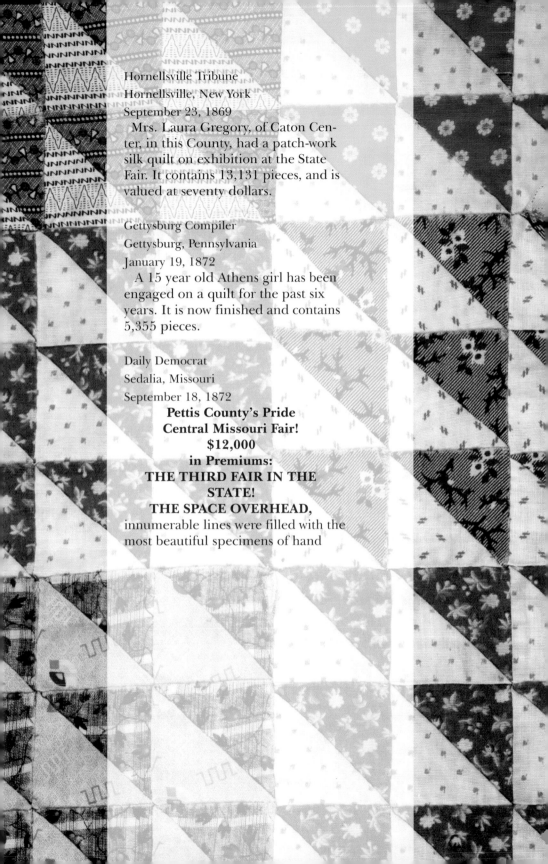

Hornellsville Tribune
Hornellsville, New York
September 23, 1869

Mrs. Laura Gregory, of Caton Center, in this County, had a patch-work silk quilt on exhibition at the State Fair. It contains 13,131 pieces, and is valued at seventy dollars.

Gettysburg Compiler
Gettysburg, Pennsylvania
January 19, 1872

A 15 year old Athens girl has been engaged on a quilt for the past six years. It is now finished and contains 5,355 pieces.

Daily Democrat
Sedalia, Missouri
September 18, 1872

**Pettis County's Pride
Central Missouri Fair!
$12,000
in Premiums:
THE THIRD FAIR IN THE
STATE!
THE SPACE OVERHEAD,**
innumerable lines were filled with the most beautiful specimens of hand

made quilts, spreads, coverlids, and counterpanes of all kinds of material from unpretending calico to the most elegant and costly silks, and our time and space both forbid a more elaborate particularizing of the hundred elegant articles of this class on exhibition in this most over-crowded and attractive department.

This department seemed to be the center of attraction at all hours of the day, and is universally admired, and especially is the superbly beautyful quilt, containing six thousand pieces, each no larger than a nickel, each quarter sixty stitches in working in, and is the most elegant one of the kind that we have ever seen on exhibition anywhere.

Evening Gazette
Port Jervis, New York
January 28, 1873

Middletown disputes with Newburgh the honor of possessing a quilt composed of the greatest number of pieces. A correspondent of the *Mail* says: Middletown is still ahead of Newburgh on the patch work quilt question. The Newburgh quilt contains 5,665 pieces, while a young lady of this place has one containing 6,272 pieces, a difference of 607 pieces. It was made by herself, and completed before she was 13 years old.

Evening Gazette
Port Jervis, New York
November 11, 1873

**What a Little Invalid Did—Two
Deftly-formed Quilts.**

Mary Louisa Kleinstuber, a daughter of John Kleinstuber of this place, before she was eight years old pieced a quilt containing 1,945 pieces. She is not yet nine years old, and has since pieced another quilt containing 3,944 pieces. During the past two or three years she has been an invalid, and the first piece was made while she was lying upon her sick-bed, and suffering great agony most of the time.

Stevens Point Journal
Stevens Point, Wisconsin
June 6, 1874

A LADY near Peoria has set out on the mission to have the name of the United States changed to Columbia. That is a small undertaking compared with making a bed-quilt composed of 469, 874 pieces.

Stevens Point Journal
Stevens Point, Wisconsin
June 13, 1874

A BEDQUILT containing 10,922 pieces has just been achieved by Mrs. Abner Coe, of Island Pond, Vt., and the lady would like to hear of a more numerous quilt than that.

Bangor Daily Whig & Courier
Bangor, Maine
July 11, 1874
 Miss Emma Brewer, a young lady of the
city, has just completed a quilt of silk,
composed of 6,181 pieces. Each piece is
the size of a copper and is six cor-
nered. She has been six years in the man-
ufacture of this wonderful piece of fabric.
—Lewiston *Journal.*

Cambridge Jeffersonian
Cambridge, Ohio
October 1, 1874
QUAKER CITY FAIR

 P. Lochary had a quilt
50 years old which was covered
with all manner of Masonic
emblems. Mrs. Caleb Arnold,
had on the lines a patch work quilt
which had in it 9675 pieces.

Morning Oregonian
Portland, Oregon
October 12, 1874
The Linn County Fair

THE NINTH ANNIVERSARY OF THE LINN
COUNTY AGRICULTURAL SOCIETY
Fifth Day
 Amongst the fancy and other work exhibit
ed, I find many patchwork quilts some very
handsome and one made by Miss Viola Kin-
sey, containing 5,504 pieces.

Bucks County Gazette
Bristol, Pennsylvania
October 15, 1874
  The only patch-working woman that ever
got her deserts was an Ohio wife, whose husband walked off with her 15,000-piece quilt,
remarking that it would save his paying six
shillings for an army blanket for the horse.

The Daily Democrat
Sedalia, Missouri
November 1, 1874
  An Ohio woman worked for nine
years piecing a quilt, to consist of
over one thousand pieces, and when
it was completed, her hard hearted
husband took it for a horse blanket.

Steubenville Daily Herald and News
Steubenville, Ohio
February 5, 1875
  The Wautoma Argas tells of a woman 60 years old in that vicinity who
has cut and pieced 61 quilts since she
was 85 years of age, each quilt containing 569 pieces. The last quilt was
cut and pieced in less than ten days.
Besides this she has done considerable
other sewing and knitting within this
time.

Daily Free Press
Manitoba, Canada
February 15, 1875
  Mrs. Alex McKellar, of Puslinch, Ont,
has immortalized herself by completing

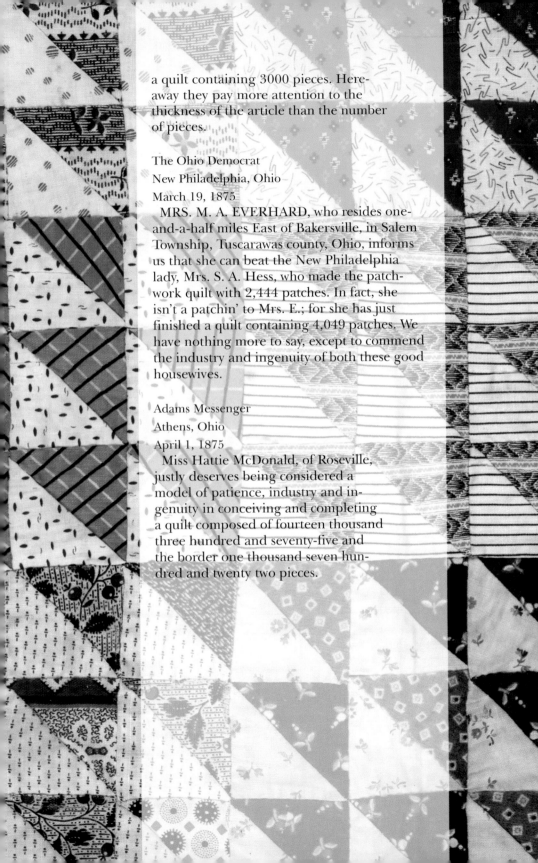

a quilt containing 3000 pieces. Here-
away they pay more attention to the
thickness of the article than the number
of pieces.

The Ohio Democrat
New Philadelphia, Ohio
March 19, 1875

MRS. M. A. EVERHARD, who resides one-
and-a-half miles East of Bakersville, in Salem
Township, Tuscarawas county, Ohio, informs
us that she can beat the New Philadelphia
lady, Mrs. S. A. Hess, who made the patchwork quilt with 2,444 patches. In fact, she
isn't a patchin' to Mrs. E.; for she has just
finished a quilt containing 4,049 patches. We
have nothing more to say, except to commend
the industry and ingenuity of both these good
housewives.

Adams Messenger
Athens, Ohio
April 1, 1875

Miss Hattie McDonald, of Roseville,
justly deserves being considered a
model of patience, industry and ingenuity in conceiving and completing
a quilt composed of fourteen thousand
three hundred and seventy-five and
the border one thousand seven hundred and twenty two pieces.

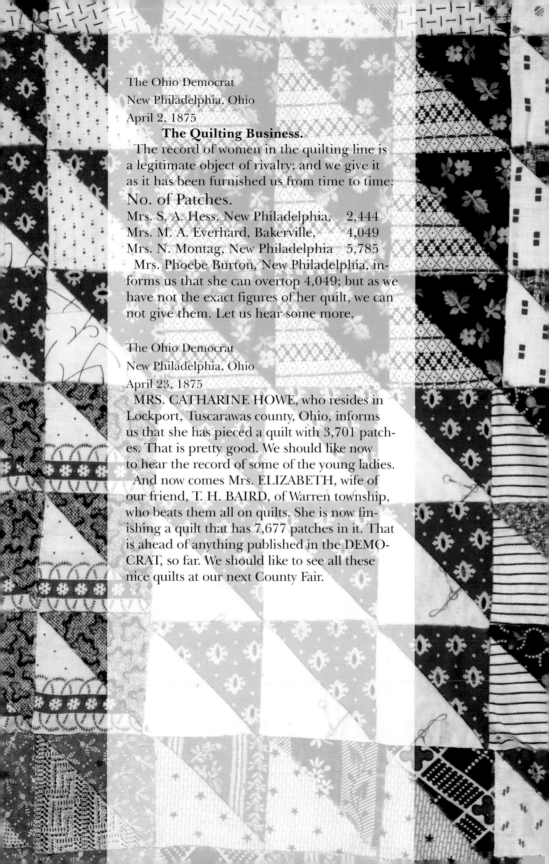

The Ohio Democrat
New Philadelphia, Ohio
April 2, 1875

The Quilting Business.

The record of women in the quilting line is a legitimate object of rivalry; and we give it as it has been furnished us from time to time:

No. of Patches.

Mrs. S. A. Hess, New Philadelphia,   2,444
Mrs. M. A. Everhard, Bakerville,   4,049
Mrs. N. Montag, New Philadelphia   5,785

Mrs. Phoebe Burton, New Philadelphia, informs us that she can overtop 4,049; but as we have not the exact figures of her quilt, we can not give them. Let us hear some more.

The Ohio Democrat
New Philadelphia, Ohio
April 23, 1875

MRS. CATHARINE HOWE, who resides in Lockport, Tuscarawas county, Ohio, informs us that she has pieced a quilt with 3,701 patches. That is pretty good. We should like now to hear the record of some of the young ladies.

And now comes Mrs. ELIZABETH, wife of our friend, T. H. BAIRD, of Warren township, who beats them all on quilts. She is now finishing a quilt that has 7,677 patches in it. That is ahead of anything published in the DEMOCRAT, so far. We should like to see all these nice quilts at our next County Fair.

THOUSANDS OF PYRAMIDS, quilt top, c.1865, cotton, 60 x 80 inches, 4,718 pieces. This quilt is in the collection of Barbara Garrett, Pottstown, Pennsylvania.

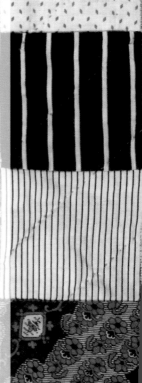

The Ohio Democrat
New Philadelphia, Ohio
May 6, 1875

ANOTHER QUILT.—Mrs. Catharine Howe
must be one of the most industrious of women. She reports another bed quilt, containing 7,066 pieces. This if we are not mistaken,
beats all the quilts yet reported. Of course,
we have not seen any of these quilts; and
make the reports just as we get them, not
doubting their correctness. Who comes next?

The Ohio Democrat
New Philadelphia, Ohio
May 27, 1875

STITCH.—Now come ladies of Knox county to dispute the question of numbers in
quilt patchwork with ladies of Tuscarawas.
The Mt. Vernon *Banner* of May 22d, says

The Tuscarawas County ladies will have to
"knock under" in this business of multi-
plying the pieces of calico in a quilt. Miss
Jennie Boum, of Danville, this county, has
completed a quilt, whose pieces number
7,850. Who can beat it?

Athens Messenger
Athens, Ohio
July 8, 1875

Last Wednesday a number of ladies,
of the M.E. Church, went to the par-
sonage, and with baskets well filled,
stayed all day and completed a quilt
that they had been piecing. The quilt
contained three thousand five hundred
and fifty pieces. It was a complete
surprise and a happy one to Mr. and
Mrs. Morgan. – (McArthur Record.

Burlington Hawk Eye
Burlington, Iowa
August 5, 1875
   Miss Laura B. Shugart, aged fifteen, and
Miss Malinda Overturf, aged twelve,
of Tama county, have each just
finished a quilt containing 10,696
pieces, and the local paper proudly asks if
anybody in Iowa can beat this? We haven't
anything in Burlington like that in the quilt
line, but Casper Cruger, up on Eighth street,
fell down the plank walk steps, leading
down to Valley street, yesterday morning,
and ran 10,697 pine slivers into the calf of
his back and vicinity, and a Tama man than
he was when he got up you never saw.

Morning Oregonian
Portland, Oregon
August 9, 1875
   By industry and preseverance a woman
can make a quilt from 21,963 pieces. Such
a thing has been done in Georgia, after
years of labor, and the quilt is as good in
all respects as one made from one piece in
a single day.

Athens Messenger
Athens, Ohio
August 26, 1875
   A colored lady, Mrs. Viney, living
in the village of Porter, has pieced a
quilt with 33,724 different pieces in it.

Coshocton Age
Coshocton, Ohio
August 26, 1875
                and
Steubenville Daily Herald and News
Steubenville, Ohio
September 10, 1875
  Emma Schott, of Roscoe, proposes to
exhibit a quilt at the Coshocton county
fair, containing 2,630 pieces or
patches.

The Ohio Democrat
New Philadelphia, Ohio
September 23, 1875
  A young lady in West Bedford, Coshocton county, Miss Martha Porter, informs
the *Age* that she has a quilt containing
12,320 pieces and that she did the work all
herself. A good wife for somebody.

Athens Messenger
Athens, Ohio
September 30, 1875
  A lady from Letart township, had a
quilt on exhibition at the Fair of this
county last week that contained one
thousand squares with no two alike.

Burlington Hawk Eye
Burlington, Iowa
October 7, 1875
     AMONG THE QUILTS,
one of our favorite haunts at the fairs.
There is the usual array at the State
Fair. The quilt containing 8,507,623

stitches, made by old Mrs. McCavendish
a lady ninety-eight years old, who
reads without glasses and eats with her
knife; never had a day's sickness in her
life; never wore a bustle nor a tie-back and
doesn't believe in sewing machines, is there.
And there is one thing to be said about these
quilts that are held together by three or four
million stitches. They are always good hon-
est quilts. There is no patchwork comforter
about them. None of these things that
seem to weigh fifty pounds when you first
crawl under it, but let you wake up in the
night, shivering at the rate of thirty-five
miles an hour, frozen from your feet to your
chin, to find, on investigation, twenty-five
pounds of cotton in each end of that comforter and nothing in the middle, while the old
thing rides you for all the world like a pair
of great saddle bags. And you can fight and
tear and punch at that cotton all the rest of
the night, but you can't get it spread out
again. And these old women quilts are
never made scant, like those hospitable de-
lusions you find in the spare bed when you
go out to visit your dear uncle. When you
crawl into bed and draw it up around your
neck and under your chin, it leaves both
your feet exposed to the cold charity of an
unfeeling world, and when you bend your
knees and tuck it under your feet, your ala-
baster bust invites a chilling atmosphere to
do its worst. You cover up your chest at
first and catch a terrific cold in your head
by freezing your feet. Then you try to warm
your feet along toward midnight, and by ex-
posing your chest you work up a cough that
says "graveyard" everytime you bark.
Finally you coil up in a heap, cover both

head and feet, compress your lungs and chest and breath the poisoned air till morning and wake up with the consumption. Nor one of these tormentors that had got a small hole torn in them, into which every time you turn you thrust a toe, and either dislocate a joint or tear the hole bigger in three or four directions. Nor one of these quilts that are so much longer than they are wide that if you happen to twist one of them over you side ways, you think you have covered yourself with a bolt of muslin, stretched, clear out and only three-quarters of a yard wide. The quilt that the old lady makes is like none of these. It is as big and warm as grandma's heart. You can tuck it under your feet till it comes up to your shoulders and cram it down around your shoulders till it reaches your feet again, and you can toss and kick and roll around under it for a week before you find your way out.

The patchwork quilt is generally, but erroneously, supposed to be a family history. This is part of Aunt Susan's dress; she was an old maid, you can see at a glance; that square was pulled out of the bottom of her bag, where it had laid undisturbed for nineteen years until the children got crazy to make a quilt for the fair. That is a

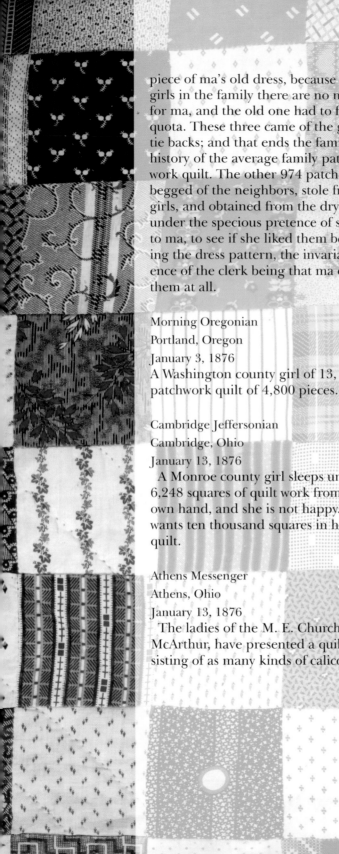

piece of ma's old dress, because with six girls in the family there are no new dresses for ma, and the old one had to furnish its quota. These three came of the girls' tie backs; and that ends the family history of the average family patch work quilt. The other 974 patches the girls begged of the neighbors, stole from other girls, and obtained from the dry goods clerks under the specious pretence of showing them to ma, to see if she liked them before ordering the dress pattern, the invariable experience of the clerk being that ma didn't like them at all.

Morning Oregonian
Portland, Oregon
January 3, 1876
A Washington county girl of 13, has made a patchwork quilt of 4,800 pieces.

Cambridge Jeffersonian
Cambridge, Ohio
January 13, 1876
  A Monroe county girl sleeps under 6,248 squares of quilt work from her own hand, and she is not happy. She wants ten thousand squares in her next quilt.

Athens Messenger
Athens, Ohio
January 13, 1876
  The ladies of the M. E. Church, of McArthur, have presented a quilt, consisting of as many kinds of calico as

possible, put together with white squares, to be kept for exhibition in 1976. It will, of course, be exhibited at different times before that. They want one thousand names on it. They have now about two hundred. All persons wishing to have their names on it, can send them to Mrs. Maria Rankin, or hand them to any of the members, always accompanied with ten cents. The dime will help support the church.-(Vinton Record.

Davenport Gazette
Davenport, Iowa
January 13, 1876
  Mrs. F. M. Peck, of Lyons, has in her possession a quaint Masonic badge, which was worn by her first husband about fifty years ago. It represents our first ancestors in the Garden of Eden gazing at the tree of life and the serpent coiled about its trunk. It is a veritable curiosity of its kind. Mrs. Peck also has a beautiful silk and velvet quilt containing 5,825 pieces.

Decatur Republican
Decatur, Illinois
February 24, 1876

A Quilt of Many Colors.—Mrs. Lillie
Crouenberg has just finished a very
handsome patch-work quilt containing
six hundred and eighty-four triangular
shaped pieces of calico, making a quilt
of the usual length and breadth. The
quilt is a very beautiful one, indeed, and
is quite a curiosity. There are no two
pieces of the patch-work of the same
color, and there is shown much taste in
the blending of the assortment for a
young married lady. We think Mrs. C.
has forever established her reputation,
and we take pleasure in complimenting
the skill of the lady in this her first at-
te.

Athens Messenger
Athens, Ohio
February 17, 1876

  Miss Mary B. Gillespie, of Adams
township, has a quilt, she calls Econ-
omy, that contains 6,668 pieces.

Davenport Daily Gazette
Davenport, Illinois
February 29, 1876

  Paul Fullmer, one of the original Old
Settlers in Le Clair township, once well
known throughout the county, but now a
resident of Marshalltown, sends this note.
  "I saw in my last week's GAZETTE an ac
count of the bed quilt containing 4,500 and
4,864 pieces, respectively. Now let Marshalltown speak, Mrs. Ida L. Jarvis, of
this city, has made a quilt containing

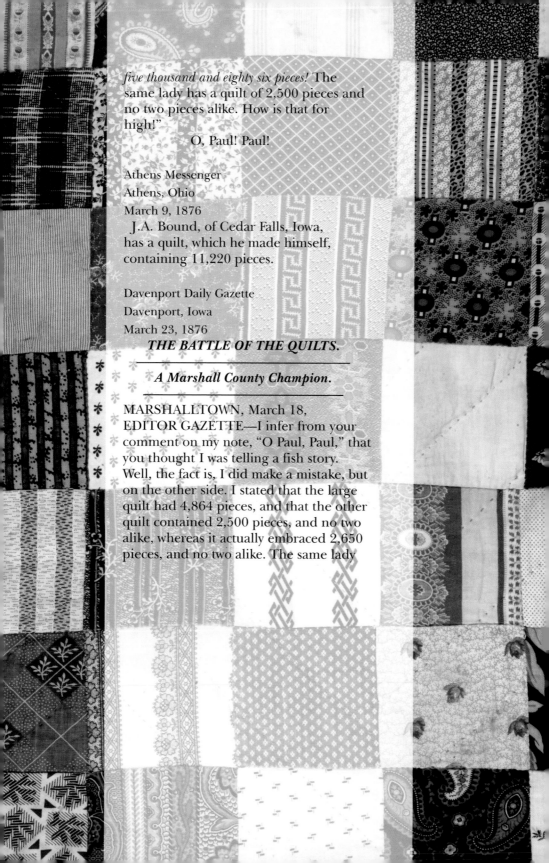

five thousand and eighty six pieces! The
same lady has a quilt of 2,500 pieces and
no two pieces alike. How is that for
high!"

       O, Paul! Paul!

Athens Messenger
Athens, Ohio
March 9, 1876
  J.A. Bound, of Cedar Falls, Iowa,
has a quilt, which he made himself,
containing 11,220 pieces.

Davenport Daily Gazette
Davenport, Iowa
March 23, 1876

THE BATTLE OF THE QUILTS.

A Marshall County Champion.

MARSHALLTOWN, March 18,
EDITOR GAZETTE—I infer from your
comment on my note, "O Paul, Paul," that
you thought I was telling a fish story.
Well, the fact is, I did make a mistake, but
on the other side. I stated that the large
quilt had 4,864 pieces, and that the other
quilt contained 2,500 pieces, and no two
alike, whereas it actually embraced 2,650
pieces, and no two alike. The same lady

Emma Willey.
1878.
1024.
Different Squares

CENTENNIAL CHARM quilt, Emma Wiley, dated 1878, cotton, 85 x 90 inches, 1,024 pieces. This quilt is in the collection of Stephanie Hatch, Boxford, Massachusetts.

CENTENNIAL quilt backing, cotton, 85 x 90 inches. This is the backing of Emma Willey's Centennial Charm quilt. The cheater cloth pattern is commonly seen in quilts made around 1876.

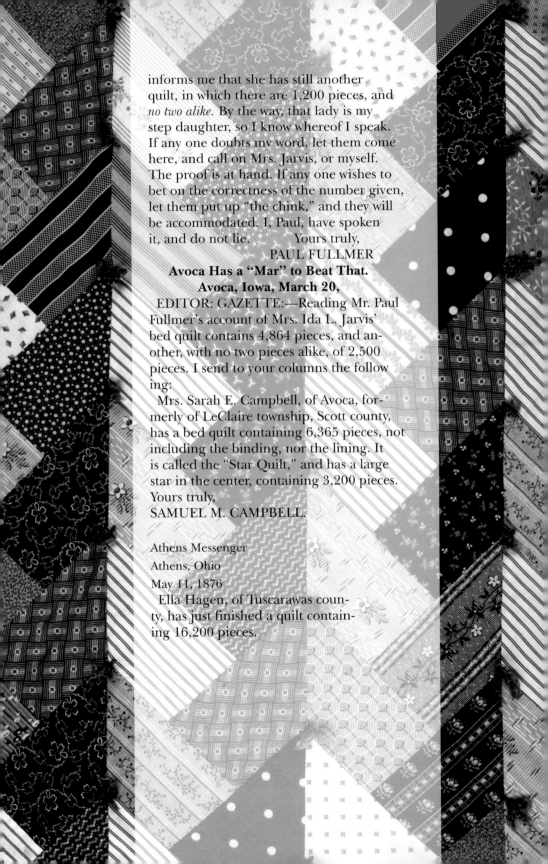

informs me that she has still another quilt, in which there are 1,200 pieces, and *no two alike*. By the way, that lady is my step daughter, so I know whereof I speak. If any one doubts my word, let them come here, and call on Mrs. Jarvis, or myself. The proof is at hand. If any one wishes to bet on the correctness of the number given, let them put up "the chink," and they will be accommodated. I, Paul, have spoken it, and do not lie.   Yours truly,

PAUL FULLMER

Avoca Has a "Mar" to Beat That.
Avoca, Iowa, March 20,

EDITOR: GAZETTE:—Reading Mr. Paul Fullmer's account of Mrs. Ida L. Jarvis' bed quilt contains 4,864 pieces, and another, with no two pieces alike, of 2,500 pieces. I send to your columns the following:

Mrs. Sarah E. Campbell, of Avoca, formerly of LeClaire township, Scott county, has a bed quilt containing 6,365 pieces, not including the binding, nor the lining. It is called the "Star Quilt," and has a large star in the center, containing 3,200 pieces. Yours truly,

SAMUEL M. CAMPBELL.

Athens Messenger
Athens, Ohio
May 11, 1876

Ella Hagen, of Tuscarawas county, has just finished a quilt containing 16,200 pieces.

Athens Messenger
Athens, Ohio
May 11, 1876
  Miss Melinda Nease, of Bowman's Run, is making a quilt which, when completed, will have 10,000 different pieces in it.

The Indiana Democrat
Indiana, Pennsylvania
May 11, 1876
  MRS. JOHN AURENTZ, of Blairsville, will send to the Centennial a quilt manufactured by herself, which contains seventeen thousand six hundred and forty separate pieces. This is some of a quilt.

Davenport Daily Gazette
Davenport, Iowa
May 27, 1876
Another Quilt Heard From.
  This one contains four thousand seven hundred and forty-three pieces, and is known as the "Beech nut pattern," and was pieced by Mrs. Jane Bowser, an old resident of this city, aged seventy-four years. The quilt was made this year. The record of its handiwork will be worthy of note among Centennial products.

The Portsmouth Times
Portsmouth, Ohio
May 27, 1876
  Miss Virginia B. Collett is piecing a quilt that will contain, when completed, ten thousand eight hundred pieces.

Davenport Gazette
Davenport, Iowa
May 30, 1876
  Here is another, and a bigger one. Mrs.
J. B. Daniels, when living in Butler township in this county, made a quilt which
contained 7,299 pieces of calico—and every piece a different figure! Come on with
your quilts! Mrs. Daniels now resides
near Montezuma, Powesheik county.

Davenport Daily Gazette
Davenport, Iowa
June 7, 1876

THE CONTEST OF QUILTS.

---

*Marshall County far Ahead – 14,109
Pieces in one Quilt.*

  Our old friend Paul Fulmer, who twenty-
eight years ago, when we became a resident of Scott county, had his name on a
snug farm about two mile above LeClaire,
on the river road, and was then numbered
among the "old settlers," sends us the following racy note, which will be read with
interest by the queens of the quilt:
  MARSHALLTOWN, June 4, 1876.
  FRIEND RUSSELL:—I suppose you think
that I am run off the course, or that my
quilt maker is dead. But not so. Since
my last the said quilt maker has been plying her needle with all her might, and,
with the assistance of her sisters, Mrs.
Freeman and Mrs. Moore, has pieced a
quilt containing 1,188 blocks, having nine
pieces to the block—10,692 pieces. In set-
ting the blocks together 3,417 pieces are
inserted, making a total of 14,109 pieces in
one quilt! So you see, friend Edward,

that Marshall county is the Banner county in
needlework as well as in everything else,
politics not excepted.

Now in conclusion, friend Edward, if
you should ever come to this neck of
woods I should be happy to have you call
and see me. But should I not be at home,
just tell my wife, Sarah Jane, that you are
the editor of the GAZETTE, and you will be
made welcome to the best the house af-
fords. We always have a supply of pork
and taters in store, except when our store
gives out. Accidents, you know, may happen in the best of families!
Yours, etc.
PAUL FULLMER.

Gazette Bulletin
Williamsport, Pennsylvania
July 3, 1876
An Allentown woman, aged 60, has
completed a quilt containing twenty-two
hundred and twenty-two pieces.

The Ohio Democrat
New Philadelphia, Ohio
August 17, 1876
MISS JOSIE GIBBS of New Philadel-
phia, has finished a quilt containing
20,008 pieces.

Athens Messenger
Athens, Ohio
August 24, 1876
Miss A.M. McIntyre, of Hocking-
port, this county, has pieced one quilt
with 5,112, pieces and another 8,175.

Evening Gazette

Port Jervis, New York

September 5, 1876

PRETTY WELL FOR AN AGED LADY.

Mrs. Anna Truex of this village, aged 83 years, has just completed a bed-quilt containing 1,838 pieces. It was pieced without the use of glasses, and was done within 30 days. It was a present for a granddaughter, a child of engineer Wm. Truex.

Daily Nevada State Journal

Reno, Nevada

September 8, 1876

MECHANICAL INGENUITY.—A little tent on the vacant lot near Hagerman's attracted considerable attention yesterday. It contained what the owners called "A Blacksmith's Dream," which is an ingenious piece of mechanism, by which puppets are made to represent every kind of employment. A quilt made of 10,000 pieces, each half an inch square is also exhibited.

The Constitution

Atlanta, Georgia

September 13, 1876

Mrs. Pickens Tate, of Cobb county, has a bed quilt with 3,668 pieces in it.

The Fitchburg Sentinel

Fitchburg, Massachusetts

September 21, 1876

As usual the show of vegetables was overhung with the specimens of needle

work by the old ladies of Leominster, which generally takes the form of bed quilts. The rage for sewing together an immense number of pieces of patchwork seems to have abated as only two specimens of this kind of perverted industry were shown. One contained 1000 pieces and was made by Mrs. Marion Derby, while the other proudly bore the inscription "1116 pieces, made by Mrs. E. F. Schragel." Another quilt, and really a handsome one was made by Mrs. Hannah Stone, 89 years of age.

Athens Messenger
Athens, Ohio
September 28, 1876
Our previous reference in the MESENGER, to exemplifications of the skill, taste and industry of Athens county ladies in the way of elaborately wrought quilts, we have reason to know, were far from exhausting that subject. We have reason to expect seeing at our County Fair, to-day and to-morrow, many additional evidences of feminine thriftiness in this department of domestic housewifery. This paragraph is prompted by having brought to our notice a quilt containing 3,246 pieces, the handiwork of aunt Fannie Courtney, of this township.

TWIST AND TURN, tied comforter, c.1880, cotton, 74 x 76 inches, 705 pieces.
This quilt is in the collection of Sue Reich, Washington Depot, Connecticut.

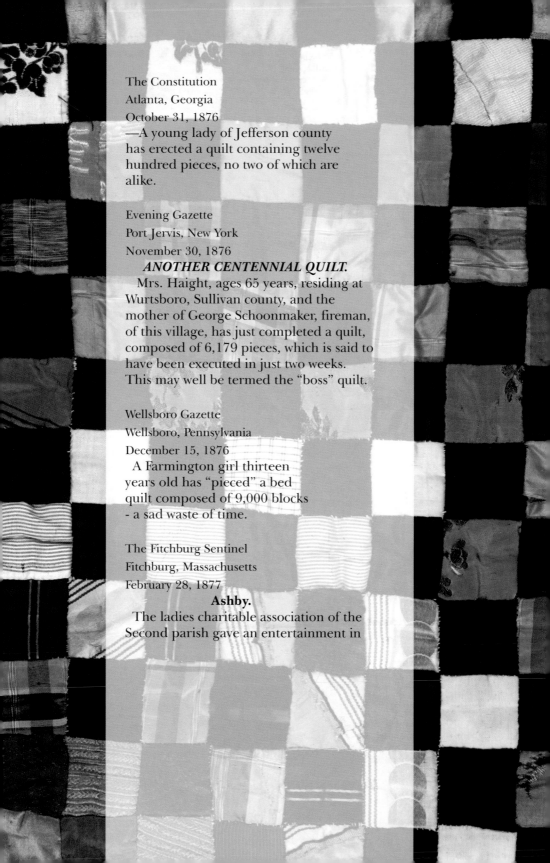

The Constitution
Atlanta, Georgia
October 31, 1876
—A young lady of Jefferson county
has erected a quilt containing twelve
hundred pieces, no two of which are
alike.

Evening Gazette
Port Jervis, New York
November 30, 1876
ANOTHER CENTENNIAL QUILT.
   Mrs. Haight, ages 65 years, residing at
Wurtsboro, Sullivan county, and the
mother of George Schoonmaker, fireman,
of this village, has just completed a quilt,
composed of 6,179 pieces, which is said to
have been executed in just two weeks.
This may well be termed the "boss" quilt.

Wellsboro Gazette
Wellsboro, Pennsylvania
December 15, 1876
   A Farmington girl thirteen
years old has "pieced" a bed
quilt composed of 9,000 blocks
- a sad waste of time.

The Fitchburg Sentinel
Fitchburg, Massachusetts
February 28, 1877
Ashby.
   The ladies charitable association of the
Second parish gave an entertainment in

the vestry of their church, Thursday evening, Feb. 22.

Tables loaded with fancy and useful articles found a ready sale. A charm bed quilt composed of 999 different pieces was received by Mrs. A. A. Smith....

Near the close of the evening F. W. Wright disposed of the articles not already not sold, at auction. The society netted about $70.

Evening Gazette

Port Jervis, New York

May 5, 1877

WONDERFUL WORK FOR AN OLD LADY.

Mrs. Nathaniel Hatch of this village, is the possessor of a bed-quilt containing 1360 pieces, the handiwork of Mrs. Sally Carter of Bristol, Putnam county, this state, who is a cousin of H. H. Farnum, esq., of this village. The lady who completed the quilt in question has already attained her nineteeth year. Who can beat this?

The Fitchburg Sentinel

Fitchburg, Massachusetts

May 11, 1877

Speaking of patchwork, a woman on Court street, has a quilt in 573,291 pieces. She spread it out in the yard to air, and a puppy dog played it was a bear. The puppy has been unwell since, and the woman spends a good deal of time in the yard waiting for him to come out from under the house. There will be some more of this item when he comes out.— (Rome Sentinel.

Evening Gazette
Port Jervis, New York
May 24, 1877
—Miss Maggie Seabold of Syracuse has completed a bed-quilt which contains 17, 160 pieces.

Indiana Democrat
Indiana, Pennsylvania
October 11, 1877
    THE quilt-makers may now come to the fore. Mrs. McKiernan, of Williamsburg, Blair county, aged 70 years, has manufactured a quilt which contains 4,640 patches. Most any sort of a person who enjoys a good conscience could sleep comfortably under such a gorgeous coverlet as the aged lady has succeeded in making.

Defiance Democrat
Defiance, Ohio
October 25, 1877
    MRS. HENRY BRUBAKER, of Wauseon, has just completed a quilt that contains 4,608 pieces.

Zanesville Daily Courier
Zanesville, Ohio
November 8, 1877
    Another silly Ohio woman has just completed a quilt containing five thousand pieces.

A woman who would spend her time over such worthless nonsense, when there is so much useful and beautiful work to be done in the world, ought to be ashamed of herself.

Evening Gazette
Port Jervis, New York
November 13, 1877
—Mrs. Norwan Seacord of Callicoon is the owner of a quilt containing 37,000 pieces.

The Daily Constitution
Atlanta, Georgia
January 2, 1878
—Mrs. Nellie Ford, of Dalton completes a quilt with 1876 pieces. Lincoln county has a slight frost.

The Daily Constitution
Atlanta, Georgia
January 5, 1878
—Telfair county is the next on the list. Mrs. Flora Grizell, sixty-one years of age, has completed a quilt which contains two thousand and sixty-four pieces.

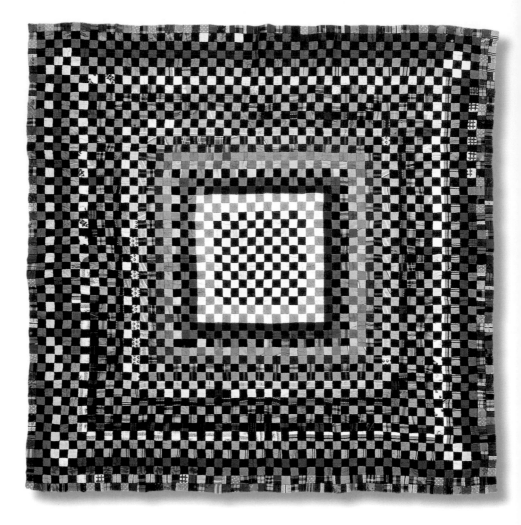

ONE PATCH SQUARE, quilt top, c.1885, silk, 50" x 51 inches, 3,080 pieces.
This quilt top belongs to Sue Reich, Washington Depot, Connecticut.

The Fresno Republican
Fresno, California
January 10, 1878
      and
Reno Evening Gazette
Reno, Nevada
January 11, 1878
   The champion time-waster is now
Rebecca Moore, who has just finished
a quilt containing 20,173 pieces.

Evening Gazette
Port Jervis, New York
March 12, 1878
—Mrs. George Ayers of Swartswood
aged 67, has made and given to her grand-
daughter a quilt containing 6,768 pieces.

Edwardsville Intelligencer
Edwardsville, Illinois
March 13, 1878
   LOG CABIN QUILT.—Miss Urath E.
Smith, an old resident of this country
informs us that she has just completed a bed-quilt, containing 364 blocks,
and that there are, in all, 8,079 pieces
in the quilt. There is a remarkable
quilt, and we await an account of the
effect it has on the first pair covered
with it.

Evening Gazette
Port Jervis, New York
April 25, 1878
ANOTHER BED QUILT OF MANY
PIECES.
   Mrs. A. B. Headley of this village has
just completed a log cabin containing

17 pieces in the block and 333 blocks in the quilt. This gives 5,661 pieces in the quilt. The work was all done by herself.

The Daily Constitution
Atlanta, Georgia
June 8, 1878
—Mrs. John Benton, of Troup county has a quilt with 7,800 pieces in it, and when completed will have about 3,000 more.

The Daily Constitution
Atlanta, Georgia
June 12, 1878
—Mrs. J. S. Barnett, of Valdosta, has a quilt in which there are over five thousand pieces, and the quilt is only about two-thirds completed.

Cambridge Jeffersonian
Cambridge, Ohio
August 1, 1878
  When a woman sighs for fame, she should let her husband cook his own meals while she makes a bed quilt with 1,000 blocks in it.

Denton Journal
Denton, Maryland
December 14, 1878
—A lady in Somerset county has just finished a bed quilt which she be-gan 52 years ago. It has 6,000 pieces.

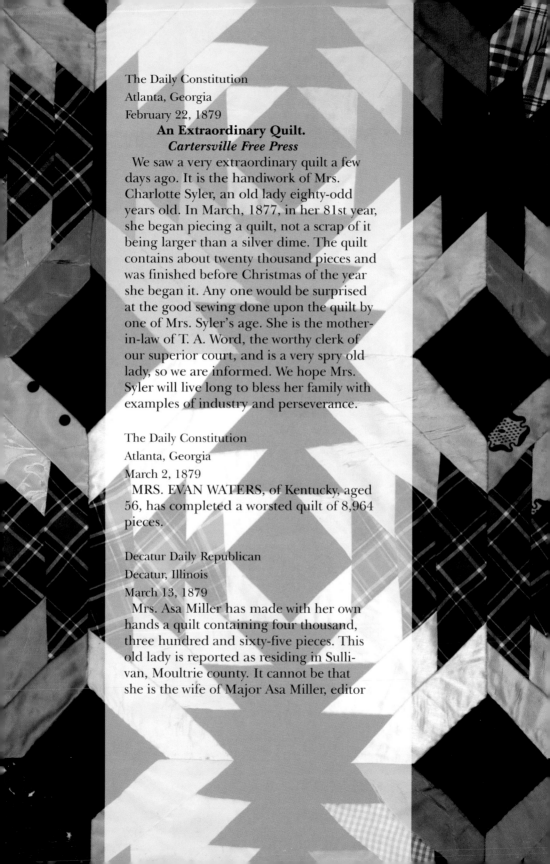

The Daily Constitution
Atlanta, Georgia
February 22, 1879

An Extraordinary Quilt.
Cartersville Free Press

We saw a very extraordinary quilt a few days ago. It is the handiwork of Mrs. Charlotte Syler, an old lady eighty-odd years old. In March, 1877, in her 81st year, she began piecing a quilt, not a scrap of it being larger than a silver dime. The quilt contains about twenty thousand pieces and was finished before Christmas of the year she began it. Any one would be surprised at the good sewing done upon the quilt by one of Mrs. Syler's age. She is the mother-in-law of T. A. Word, the worthy clerk of our superior court, and is a very spry old lady, so we are informed. We hope Mrs. Syler will live long to bless her family with examples of industry and perseverance.

The Daily Constitution
Atlanta, Georgia
March 2, 1879

MRS. EVAN WATERS, of Kentucky, aged 56, has completed a worsted quilt of 8,964 pieces.

Decatur Daily Republican
Decatur, Illinois
March 13, 1879

Mrs. Asa Miller has made with her own hands a quilt containing four thousand, three hundred and sixty-five pieces. This old lady is reported as residing in Sullivan, Moultrie county. It cannot be that she is the wife of Major Asa Miller, editor

of the Tuscola *Review*. If he has gone
and done it, he has kept it pretty shady.

The Daily Constitution
Atlanta, Georgia
April 20, 1879
—Dallas is ahead on quilts. The Marietta
Journal says Mrs. G. W. Foote has a quilt
with two thousand two hundred and ninety-
one pieces in it, pieced and quilted by herself in her fifty-ninth year. Mrs. Frank Gann
has one with two thousand two hundred
and thirty-six pieces in it, and one ready for
quilting with three thousand nine hundred
and seventy pieces in it, both made by herself.

Evening Gazette
Port Jervis, New York
April 22, 1879
   A WELL-PIECED BED-QUILT.
  We are shown Monday a bed-quilt
made by Miss Sarah S. McCarron of Roses
Point, near Cuddebackville, but now liv-
ing in Port Jervis, which contains 15,785
distinct pieces, and was made up by Miss
McCarron after school hours, when but 13
years of age. If we mistake not this takes
the lead.

Burlington Hawk Eye
Burlington, Iowa
May 8, 1879
—The Ackley *Enterprise* says that Mrs.
Sallie Hardin, an old-fashioned girl of

eighty-four, at Iowa Falls, is building her
fortieth bed quilt, each spread being
composed of two thousand diminutive and
variegated pieces of silk.

Marion Daily Star
Marion, Ohio
June 26, 1879

Patchwork.

As this old-fashioned work is again
becoming fashionable, a few remarks
about its appropriateness and utility
may not be amiss. There are some persons who have a perfect passion for this
work; there is for them a perfect fascination in arranging and placing the various
bits of color. No other kind of needle
work is as suitable for teaching a little
girl the use of the needle. It is pleasant
to see the effect of the combinations
and contrasts, and the little fingers
can work more nimbly, in the short
over and over seams, than they would
in the long seams of either pillow-cases
or sheets. It is, besides, a nice way to
make disposition of the accumulation of
remnants in the scrap-bag. Old ladies,
too, like to piece bed-quilts, and "grandmother's quilts" are precious heir-looms
in many families. It is a matter of pride
with these venerable ladies to be able to
do something that is useful and pretty;
and no doubt, many memories of the
by-gone years are stitched into the seams,
and perhaps some sad reminiscences are
called forth by the sight of a long-for-
gotten remnant of a garment, worn in
the long-ago by one whose busy hands
are placed over the pulseless heart. To

PINEAPPLE LOG CABIN quilt top, c.1890, silk, 56.5 x 62.5 inches, 1,748 pieces. This quilt top belongs to Sue Reich, Washington Depot, Connecticut.

the old ladies who delight in this work, it is doubtless a solace in many a lonely hour, and it would be almost a deed of cruelty to pronounce the labor of their hands useless. And to the little ones, who ought to learn to ply the polished shaft, it is mixing pleasure with profit. If an active, mature person has nothing else to employ idle hands and hours, it may do to cut up calico into scraps, just for the sake of keeping out of mischief; but there are so many more profitable ways of employing one's time and energy, that it seems a waste of both to spend them upon patchwork. An aged lady of my acquaintance has, within the past year, pieced together, four quilts, 30,000 pieces of cloth, and showed great taste and ingenuity in their construction; and it is really a deed of kindness to employ her to make patch-work, as it helps support her, and en-ables her to purchase many comforts with which to brighten her pathway to the grave.—*Rural New Yorker.*

Daily Constitution
Atlanta, Georgia
October 7, 1879
—The Quitman Reporter says that Jacob Small, an old colored man living on the road from Quitman to Grooverville, exhib-ted in that office last Saturday a patch quilt put together by his wife, Dicy Small, aged 52 years, and which contained 1,314 pieces. Jacob is himself 67 years old, and says he was brought to Brooks county when

quite young—when Brooks was a frontier country and Indians could be seen here every day—and has been here ever since. Since the war he has managed to buy a small place and settle himself and wife upon it, and emigrant agents hunting up emigrants for Kansas could not offer him a greater insult than to talk to him about leaving it and going to Kansas or anywhere else.

Morning Oregonian
Portland, Oregon
October 27, 1879
   Mrs. Huntington, aged 70, shows a patchwork
quilt of several thousand or more pieces….

Cambridge Jeffersonian
Cambridge, Ohio
November 20, 1879
   Mrs. George Walker is our champion quilt piecer. She has finished a quilt which has 3250 different pieces in it.

Defiance Democrat
Defiance, Ohio
April 29, 1880
   Mrs. Caroline Patent has a quilt containing 5,000 patches all different kinds.

The Daily Constitution
Atlanta, Georgia
April 30, 1880
—Cartersville Free Press: Mrs. Siler,

mother of Mrs. Thomas A. Word, of this place, is one of the most remarkable old ladies we have ever known. She is now 82 or 83 years old, and is sprightly and active as a woman of fifty. She is exceedingly industrious, and is seldom idle. She says when she is not employed she does not know what to do with her hands. She has on hand now about twenty quilts in patchwork ready to be quilted. We remarked to her that she ought to have occasional quiltings and get all the young ladies to help her do the work, but she replied that she was afraid the girls would spoil her work. Her patch-work is exceedingly beautiful, displaying great taste in patterns and exquisite neatness in sewing. She has just completed a quilt of hers last fall with over ten thousand pieces in it. It was quilted with great care. That piece of work she sent to the fair at Macon last fall, and we supposed she was certain of a premium upon it; but what was our surprise when we heard that she not only failed to be recognized but the quilt was not even mentioned as an article of merit. It was a shame.

Cambridge Jeffersonian
Cambridge, Ohio
June 3, 1880
   Mrs. Sarah Forsythe, who lives with the family of Isaac Smith of this place, and is now past seventy-eight years of age, has a quilt which she commenced in 1836 and finished in 1841 which contains seven thousand one hundred fifty-three pieces.

She is the widow of Elijah Forsythe, who died near New Concord some years ago.

Cambridge Jeffersonian
Cambridge, Ohio
June 17, 1880
  Carrie Swan, of Newcomerstown, has quilted a quilt with 11,664 squares.

Chester Daily Times
Chester, Pennsylvania
June 17, 1880
  Binghamton *Republican:* The woman who makes a bed quilt containing twenty thousand pieces, and the man who crowds fourteen thousand words on a postal card, have fulfilled their missions in this world, and should be persuaded either to kindle a fire with coal oil or experiment with a flying machine.

Morning Oregonian
Portland, Oregon
July 6, 1880
  Mrs. E. Reilly comes in with a patchwork quilt that discounts the one of 4942 pieces, before noticed by 2058 pieces. The work is also much more neatly executed, perhaps by more mature hands, and if the two compete the blue ribbon will doubtless ornament the one of 7000 pieces.

Evening Gazette

Port Jervis, New York

July 17, 1880

A SMART OLD LADY.
AGED 82 YEARS AND AS ACTIVE AS MANY OF 40 – THE BED QUILT SHE HAS PIECED.

On passing Wood's Eagle hotel on Front street, one frequently notices a pleasant-faced old lady, occupying her customary seat near the parlor window, and always engaged with her knitting or the needle.

She is the mother of W. H. Wood, Supervisor of Wawayanda and also of our townsman S. J. Woods.

The weighty burden of 82 years appears to sit lightly upon her, and her step is as firm and elastic as it was a half a century ago. Her mental facilities are unimpaired and she converses understandably of occurrences beyond the ken of the present generation. She takes her daily walk about the village streets, and when at home is constantly employed in some light house-hold affairs.

She has just finished a quilt, of the pattern known as the "Court House Steps" work is handsomely done, and would be a credit to a person of a fifth her years.

Verily old father time has dealt kindly with the old lady.

Daily Constitution

Atlanta, Georgia

September 3, 1880

Miss Anne Conway, of Millersburg, Ky., has just finished a silk quilt which has 926 pieces.

Chester Daily Times
Chester, Pennsylvania
October 8, 1880
   LARGE QUILT.—Mrs. Mary Garsed, of
Rockdale, has made a quilt which contains
15,894 pieces.

Cambridge Jeffersonian
Cambridge, Ohio
October 21, 1880
   Mrs. David Hosfelt beats all the other
housewives at cutting up calico and
sewing it together again. Her last quilt
contains 20,000 pieces.

Daily Kennebec Journal
Augusta, Maine
December 20, 1880
   Mrs. C. F. Beals of Auburn, distances all
competitors on quilts. She has one quilt containing 1806 pieces, and two quilts in each
of which are 5,693 pieces.

Gettysburg Compiler
Gettysburg, Pennsylvania
March 24, 1881
   A quilt made at West Point, Ga., con-
tains 21,936 pieces.

Cambridge Jeffersonian
Cambridge, Ohio
March 25, 1881
   Mrs. Solomon Mercer presented her
son, S. W., with a quilt containing two

thousand six hundred and forty pieces. It was pieced by her thirty-six years ago.

Athens Messenger
Athens, Ohio
March 31, 1881

Mrs. O. A. Patterson, formerly of this place, but now of Hallsville, Ross county, has two patchwork quilts, made by her own hands within a year, one containing 9,036 separate pieces of calico, the other 8,444. She is 72 years old and in very delicate health, and only sews those bits of calico together to pass away time, but they are curiosities.

The Globe
Atchison, Kansas
April 4, 1881

The annual quilt story lie is now on its travels. This time it is an old lady named Miss Kate Smith, blind from infancy, who has made a quilt containing 55,550 pieces. She worked on this quilt three years; used 100 spools of thread, and threaded every needle herself. Miss Smith is an inmate of the Union Home for aged ladies in Philadelphia, and the *Press*, of that city, vouches for the truth of this seeming improbable feat.

Evening Gazette
Port Jervis, New York
May 12, 1881

Lucy A. Tompkins of Lord's Gate has just finished piecing a remarkable bed quilt. It consists of 16,865 pieces, and the harmony of light and shade is perfect.

Athens Messenger
Athens, Georgia
May 19, 1881

Miss Kate Lake, of Plymouth, this County, aged 81, has, says the Marietta Register, recently, finished a quilt, after 8 months' work containing 4,368 pieces.

Cambridge Jeffersonian
Cambridge, Ohio
May 19, 1881

BRIDGEVILLE.

Mrs. May Robinson, formerly of Wheeling township, has pieced a quilt containing 1986 pieces. Who, of our old ladies, can beat this?

The Globe
Atchinson, Kansas
June 24, 1881

The quilt patchwork paragrapher is getting in his work again. He tells of a Miss Belle Redman, of Dubuque, Iowa, aged 104, who lately finished a quilt which contained 10,049 pieces, and who is now at work on another quilt which will be composed of 7,000 pieces.

NINE PATCH quilt top, c.1885, cotton, 63 x 65.5 inches, 5,175 pieces.
This quilt top is in the collection of Sue Reich, Washington Depot, Connecticut.

Wellsboro Agitator
Wellsboro, Pennsylvania
June 21, 1881
—Mrs. Levi Brown, of Lawrenceville
has made a bed quilt this year containing
nearly 11 000 pieces of cloth. Such work
as that looks like a sad waste of time.

Evening Gazette
Port Jervis, New York
July 21, 1881
  Mrs. Everts, mother of Mrs. S.S.
Masten of this place, has made a quilt
with over 8,000 small pieces, of many
colors. This shows considerable pa-
tience for a lady of 83 years.

The Globe
Atchinson, Kansas
September 29. 1881
Exposition Notes
  Mrs. L. K. Wells, a Garden of Eden quilt, a
complete panorama of the rise and fall of
the first family; Mrs. Harris, an album
quilt one hundred years old, composed of
3,682 pieces; Mrs. Richard Clark, a silk
quilt of 5,000 pieces, and many other ladies
articles of equal merit. We congratulate
those having it in charge for their taste.

Athens Messenger
Athens, Ohio
October 13, 1881
  Mrs. Elmer Gabriel, of Waterloo
township, is credited with the possession of a quilt containing 16,400 pieces,
all her own handiwork.

Allen County Democrat
Lima, Ohio
January 12, 1882
    A Hardin county lady, Miss
Raines, has made a quilt containing
6,527 pieces.

Freeborn County Standard
Albert Lea, Minnesota
March 2, 1882
        and
Allen County Democrat
Lima, Ohio
March 9, 1882
    Vermont has a model farmer. He does
his own work on the farm, and spends his
winter evenings at knitting and sewing.
His evening work so far this winter consists
of four pairs of double mittens, a quilt,
containing 928 pieces and one containing
1,225 pieces, and he is engaged on another
calico mosaic.

Gettysburg Compiler
Gettysburg, Pennsylvania
March 15, 1882
    Miss Addie E. Jacobs, Huntington
township, has a quilt of 24,122 patches.

Gettysburg Compiler
Gettysburg, Pennsylvania
April 5, 1882
    Miss Clara Stevens's new quilt has
6,552 patches. Huntington township
ahead.

Defiance Democrat
Defiance, Ohio
April 13, 1882
   Lizzie Grossell has just completed a
worsted quilt containing 3,852 pieces.

Democrat
Olean, New York
April 18, 1882
   The latest bed-quilt fiend turns up in
Rushford. Her name is Alice Davis, and
she is over 80 years old. During the last
five years she has pieced thirty-nine bed-
quilts and three of the same since her last
birthday. Three of the thirty-nine contained 6,000 pieces, and the remaining
thirty-six from 1,300 to 5,000 pieces.

Gettysburg Compiler
Gettysburg, Pennsylvania
April 19, 1882
   Miss Annie E. Biddle, of White
Hall, has just finished a quilt with 7,650
patches.

Gettysburg Compiler
Gettysburg, Pennsylvania
April 26, 1882
   Mrs. John Lauver, of Butler township,
has a quilt which contains 8,424 patches.

Gettysburg Compiler
Gettysburg, Pennsylvania
May 3, 1882
   ADAMS COUNTY has become an impor-

tant manufacturing centre. Miss Annie Biddle, of White House, that county, has just finished a quilt with 7,650 patches. Miss Amanda Dutterer, of Menallen township, that county, has one made with 6,800 patches. Several townships are yet to hear from.—*Valley Spirit.* Just as though nothing but "Taylor Works" was worth talking about.

Daily Kennebec Journal
Augusta, Maine
September 6, 1882

We notice on exhibition in Miss H. E. Piper's window a beautiful silk quilt of the kaleidoscope pattern, made by the ladies of the Unitarian society, which contains three or four thousand separate pieces. It is worth $50, and some one will get it for 50 cents. One hundred shares are to be sold, and the buyers will have an opportunity to draw for the possession of the gorgeous coverlid, the one drawing the slip marked "quilt" to carry off the prize.

Cambridge Jeffersonian
Cambridge, Ohio
September 7, 1882

The industry of our young ladies is noticeable in the fact that Miss Anna E. Scott has just completed a quilt which contains 7,550 pieces.

Defiance Democrat
Defiance, Ohio
January 25, 1883
A Trumbull county
woman of 85 has just completed a quilt
with nearly 5,000 pieces in it.

Athens Messenger
Athens, Ohio
February 8, 1883
   The Lowell Courier says an East
Brookfield woman, aged sixty-six years
boasts of having made a patchwork
quilt containing two million pieces. It
is not stated what she did between
whiles, but we don't believe she made
many speeches at woman's rights con-
ventions. A Norristown woman, aged
eighty-eight years, and blind, has just
finished a quilt, begun three years ago,
containing 643,274,610,598,000 pieces.
One of these items may be a little more
difficult to believe than the other, but
not much. (Norristown Herald.

Allen City Democrat
Lima, Ohio
February 8, 1883
—The fool killer should be let loose
on the woman who has pieced a quilt
containing 36,000 pieces.

Gettysburg Compiler
Gettysburg, Pennsylvania
March 7, 1883
   An Ohio woman has pieced a quilt con-

taining 36,000 pieces. This beats the one
mentioned in the Compiler a few weeks
ago.

Olean Democrat
Olean, New York
March 27, 1883

AT THE GREAT STATE FAIR AT JACKSONVILLE.
An Interesting and well Written Account of What an Olean Man Saw and Heard.

The usual five thousand piece
bed quilt, the one made by the octo-
generian lady without spectacles,
also the one made of silk samples
sponged from New York dealers,
were all there, but not closely exam-
ined.

Hopewell Herald
Hopewell, New Jersey
April 18, 1883

Mrs. Mary H. Stites, of Deerfield
township, Cumberland county, has
finished a bed quilt containing ten
thousand five hundred and fifty pieces.

Gettysburg Compiler
Gettysburg, Pennsylvania
April 25, 1883

Mrs. Mary A. Hauptman, living near
this place, has a quilt containing 5,530
patches.

Trenton Times
Trenton, New Jersey
May 31, 1883
  Miss Tille Pimm, near Flemington, has a
bed-quilt, of her own make, which contains
5,760 blocks, each 4 1/8 inch square.

Newark Daily Advocate
Newark, Ohio
November 6, 1883
Wonderful Bed Quilts.
(Press Iterus.)
  A Georgia woman has just finished a silk
quilt containing 2,400 pieces, and over 1,000
yards of thread.
    Miss Allie Martin, of Lusby's Mill, Ky.,
has a quilt containing 4,863 blocks each three-
quarters of an inch square.
    Mrs. M. Baker, of Lone Tree, Iowa, has a
quilt upon which she has been at work seven
years, in which is worked the solar system.
She made a trip to Chicago to view the
comet and sun spots through the telescope
that she might locate them accurately.
    Miss Allie Martin, of Lesley's Mills, made
a quilt containing 4,863 pieces, and the local
editor challenged the state to beat it. Miss
Allie Gorham, of Paris, came to the front
with a composite bed covering constructed
out of 7,048 individual bits of calico, and she
is now the champion.

The Landmark
Statesville, North Carolina
March 7, 1884
  Mr. P. W. Eagle, of Ohio township,
the other day counted the pieces in a

quilt which he bought some time ago from a mountain woman, and found that they numbered 3,655. Who beats this?

The Landmark
Statesville, North Carolina
March 14, 1884

The Quilt Business

The gentleman from Coddle Creek (Mr. R.S. Brown) presents his compliments to the gentleman from Ohio, (Mr. P. W. Eagle), and invites him to take a back seat on his mountain quilt with 3,655 pieces. The Widow Nancy Brown, of Coddle Creek, has one with 6,561 pieces. Mr. Eagle seems to be defeated by a large majority.

And in addition to this Mrs. J. P. Lentz, of Locke's township, Rowan county, writes that she has a quilt of her own make which has in it 3,804 pieces.

We will now proceed to close the polls.

Stevens Point Journal
Stevens Point, Wisconsin
March 29, 1884

A certain girl has pieced a "crazy quilt" containing 9,000 bits of ribbon. It must have taken at least three minutes sewing to the piece. That would make 27,000 minutes-an hour a day for a year and nearly three months. In that time this foolish girl might have learned a modern language, became an accomplished cook and housekeeper,

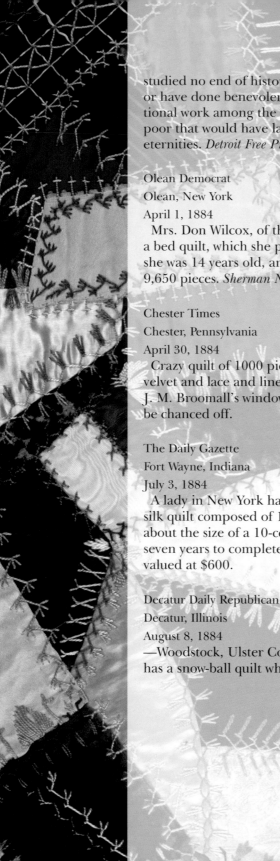

studied no end of history and science, or have done benevolent and educational work among the ignorant and poor that would have lasted to the eternities. *Detroit Free Press*

Olean Democrat
Olean, New York
April 1, 1884
  Mrs. Don Wilcox, of this town, has a bed quilt, which she pieced before she was 14 years old, and it contains 9,650 pieces. *Sherman News*

Chester Times
Chester, Pennsylvania
April 30, 1884
  Crazy quilt of 1000 pieces, edged with velvet and lace and lined with satin, in J. M. Broomall's window on Saturday, to be chanced off.

The Daily Gazette
Fort Wayne, Indiana
July 3, 1884
  A lady in New York has finished a silk quilt composed of 14,000 pieces, each about the size of a 10-cent piece. It took her seven years to complete this work, and it is valued at $600.

Decatur Daily Republican
Decatur, Illinois
August 8, 1884
—Woodstock, Ulster County, N.Y. has a snow-ball quilt which is a curiosity.

It consists of 7,650 pieces, and is the handiwork of a young lady named Miss I. Shultis.

Stevens Point Journal
Stevens Point, Wisconsin
August 9, 1884
  The girl with soft gray eyes and rippling brown hair, who walked all over your poor, fluttering heart at the charity ball, has just finished a crazy quilt containing 1,064 pieces of neckties and hat-linings, put together with 21,390 stitches. And her poor old father fastens on his suspenders with a long nail, a piece of twine, a sharp stick, and one regularly ordained button.—*Burlington Hawkeye.*

The Wellsboro Agitator
Wellsboro, Pennsylvania
August 19, 1884
—Mrs. S. M. Curran, of Deerfield is 78 years old. The *Courier* is authority for the statement that she has just pieced a bed-quilt of 1,440 pieces. Since July, 1883, she has pieced thirteen quilts, and in the past fifteen years she has pieced fifty.

The Daily News
Butte, Montana
September 20, 1884
  This is the way an exchange speaks for the lady candidate for the Presidency: "If it takes ten minutes to add on scrap to a 'crazy quilt' of

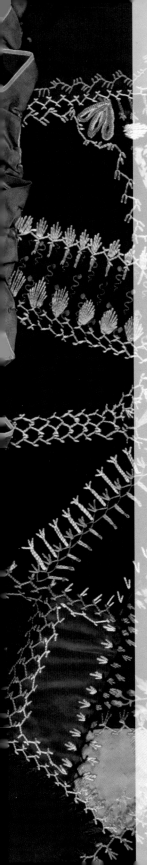

9,000 pieces, the completed work represents an outlay of 1,500 hours. That time devoted to the advocacy of Belva A. Lockwood for the Presidency would win for her many votes. Shall the ladies of this country let slip such a chance to place at the head of the nation one of their own sex? Never! Every lady in the land should lay aside her crazy-quilt patchwork and enlist in the army of fair warriors for the beautiful Belva."

The Daily Gazette
Fort Wayne, Indiana
November 12, 1884
  A BRIDGEPORT woman who cut her dress from a New York *Herald* war map, thinking it was a *Harper's Bazar* pattern, discovered her error before she finished the robe, but she went ahead and sewed the pieces together, and now she has a crazy quilt of 2,000 pieces which is the envy of all her female friends.—*Norristown Herald.*

Hornellsville Weekly Tribune
Hornellsville, New York
November 28, 1884
  Miss Ada Nicholson, of Hornellsville, has just finished a quilt containing 3,591 pieces.

Defiance Democrat
Defiance, Ohio
January 1, 1885
—Miss Eliza Kidd, of Keene, Ky., is

only twenty years of age, but has immortalized herself by finishing a crazy
quilt containing 58,841 pieces, 562,897
stitches, 21 spools of thread, and 30 yards
of cloth.

The Wellsboro Agitator
Wellsboro, Pennsylvania
January 20, 1885
—Miss Nettie Springer of Homer Potter
county has just completed a silk crazy
quilt containing 5,700 pieces....

Morning Oregonian
Portland, Oregon
May 10, 1885
  Mrs. Dr. Hunt has received from Providence,
R.I., a silk bed-quilt containing 2500 pieces.
The quilt is in log cabin pattern, made by
hand, and is the work of the mother of Dr.
Hunt, a lady now in her 86th year.

The Daily Northwestern
Oshkosh, Wisconsin
June 5, 1885
  Miss Ella F. Kidd of Keane, Ky.,
has just completed a crazy quilt which
contains 100,000 pieces and 948,688
stitches.

Atchison Globe
Atchison, Kansas
June 16, 1885
Examples of Patience.
(Puck.)

St. Nicholas says that "the number of years the Esquimaux will spend in plodding away at the most simple things shows them to be probably the most patient people in the world." Now, what we wish to say is that, no matter how patient these people may be, we don't think they would have patience to stand on a front stoop at 2 o'clock in the morning, with a stiff breeze blowing, and pick the overcoat lining out for a nightkey when the darkness made it impossible to see the key. We also think they would not have the patience to put 8,917,987 pieces of silk into a crazy quilt, to be given to a church fair for nothing.

The Daily Gazette
Fort Wayne, Indiana
June 30, 1885
A GOOD REASON.
Why does she hold her head so high
And look so supercilious,
And pass the other maidens by
As if they made her bilious
Well may she proudly walk the street,
The while her pride increases;
Her crazy quilt is just complete
Made of ten thousand pieces.
—*Boston Courier*

Stevens Point Gazette
Stevens Point, Wisconsin
November 28, 1885
Among the entries for the crazy-quilt

CRAZY Quilt, c.1885, silk, satin, velvet, 47 x 58 inches.
This quilt is in the collection of Sue Reich, Washington Depot, Connecticut.

show held in New York recently was
one made by a soldier of pieces taken
from the uniforms of distinguished of-
ficers to the number of 8,700 pieces,
and which required two and a half
years to make. It is valued at $3,000.
One quilt is made of 17,000 pieces.

The New Era
Humeston, Iowa
December 3, 1885
One of the curiosities at a church fair
in Unionville was a quilt containing
9,638.

The Wellsboro Agitator
Wellsboro, Pennsylvania
March 30, 1886

Purely Personal

**INTERESTING FACTS CONCERNING
PROMINENT PEOPLE.**

Mrs. Julia Smith, of Glastonbury, Conn.,
recently deceased, bequeathed the famous
Jersey cows to her husband, but of her
other personal property she gave to Mrs.
Jane H. Sheppard of the Riggs. House,
Washington, "my silk bedquilt, containing 7,000 pices, to Mrs. James Noble of
Westfield, Mass., the Wallingford table-
cloth without the seam, spun by myself and
sister, and the 120 year-old bed-quilt of
dimity made by my grandmother before
her marriage, who spun and wove the lining and quilted the same.

The New Era
Humeston, Iowa
April 1, 1886
   Mrs. N. J. Burk, of Grundy Center,
has just completed a worsted quilt
which contains 11,207 separate pieces.
Some time ago she finished a calico quilt
containing 7,703 pieces.

Daily Nevada State Journal
Reno, Nevada
July 31, 1887
   A young lady in Eagle Valley, Ormsby
County, has made a bed quilt contain-
ing 16,000 pieces less than the size of a
man's thumb nail. Pass this around.

Daily Nevada State Journal
Reno, Nevada
August 7, 1887
   An exchange some time ago stated
that a Douglas county girl had made a
bed quilt out of 16,000 thumb nails or
run 16,000 bed quilts into a thumb nail,
or something to that effect. It was an
important item and should have been
copied.

Semi Weekly Age
Coshocton, Ohio
September 14, 1887
   Henry Worthington, of Geneseo, Ill.,
is a young man who is willing to have
his name go sounding down the aisles
of time as the author and finisher of a

mosaic quilt containing 6,022 pieces. During the long, cold evenings of last winter, while the other young fellows were having a good time with their best girls, Henry remained quietly at home and assiduously stitched away at his quilt.

Daily Nevada State Journal
Reno, Nevada
September 16, 1887

  THE CRAZY QUILT,—Rev. Mrs. C. L. Fisher will compete for Jack Frazier's prize of $10.00 for a crazy quilt. She is now over 65 years of age. The quilt will contain 2,018 pieces of silk and satin. Mrs. Fisher will contend for Mr. Pownings prize offered for the grand medal on the basis that she will exhibit a ladies silk shawl which was built in 1762 and which is still in a perfect state of preservation. The lady will wear this old reminder at the Fair after the prize has been awarded her.

Denton Journal
Denton, Maryland
October 8, 1887

  A Florida woman has made a bed quilt containing 16,000 pieces less than the size of a man's thumb.

CRAZY Quilt, c.1885, silk, satin, velvet, 67 x 75 inches.
This quilt is in the collection of Sue Reich, Washington Depot, Connecticut.

Marion Weekly Star
Marion, Ohio
October 15, 1887
  Mr. Benjamin Atwood, of this county, has
a little daughter 12 years old, who is quite an
exception. She has just completed a quilt
which contains 2,176 pieces. She has a very
good literary education, as well as, extensive
knowledge of household duties. The first day
she picked cotton this season she gathered 111
pounds, sea island, which is more than double
per weight. – Excelsior (Ga.) Eagle.

Athen Messenger
Athens, Ohio
November 17, 1887
  A YOUNG lady in Missouri has a collection of 17,653 spools. This hobby is
far ahead of the crazy quilt mania, and
more useful than decorating china with
flowers unknown to botanical science.
The young man who shall link his des-
tiny with this girl will have a soft soap
on kindling wood.

Olean Democrat
Olean, New York
December 1, 1887
          and
Marion Weekly Star
Marion, Ohio
December 17, 1887
  Lizzie Bell Sinclair, of Everittstown, N. J.
celebrated her twelfth birthday recently by
completing a bed quilt that contains 11,210
pieces.

Gettysburg Compiler
Gettysburg, Pennsylvania
January 3, 1888
  MISS LILLIAN DAY, of York Springs, has
made a quilt with between 25,000 and 28,
000 pieces.

Marion Weekly Star
Marion, Ohio
February 25, 1888
  Miss Eunice Hooser, of Elkton, Ky., has
just completed a calico quilt that is composed
of 24,080 pieces, and the local newspapers
say that she is not only a skillful needle-
woman, but one of the prettiest young ladies
in the country.

Morning Oregonian
Portland, Oregon
March 7, 1888
  A young lady at Heyworth, Ill., has made a
crazy-quilt with 28,062 pieces in it, and it's dollars to doughnuts that her husband – if she ever
has one – will want to pin his coat-tails to his
trousers for want of a single patch.– Minneapolis Tribune.

The Landmark
Statesville, North Carolina
March 8, 1888
  A number of the relatives and friends
of Master Junius Mott Plyler met at
the residence of his grandfather, Mr.
Hugh Plyler, last Wednesday, to cel-
brate the twelfth anniver-no, that
won't do. It is not the twelfth. I will

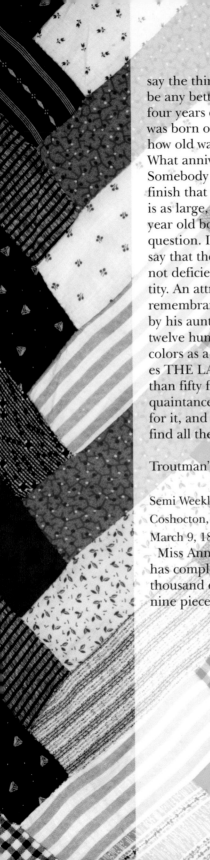

say the third then; but that will not
be any better, for what comes every
four years cannot be called that. He
was born on February 29, 1876. Now,
how old was he February 29th, 1888?
What anniversary of his birth was it?
Somebody do tell me, and then how to
finish that unfinished sentence. He
is as large, stout and sensible as a 12-
year old boy, but is he that old? is the
question. I need no help, however, to
say that the dinner there that day was
not deficient either in quality or quan-
tity. An attraction of the day was a
remembrance quilt top, put together
by his aunt, Mrs. Mary Williamson, of
twelve hundred pieces and as many
colors as a meadow in bloom. He wishes THE LANDMARK to thank the more
than fifty friends, relatives and ac-
quaintances who contributed the stars
for it, and to assure them that he can
find all their names somewhere on it.
        LaF.
Troutman's N. C. March 5th, 1888

Semi Weekly Age
Coshocton, Ohio
March 9, 1888
  Miss Anna Spragg of Adamsville
has completed a quilt containing five
thousand eight hundred and forty
nine pieces.

Weekly News
Frederick, Maryland
April 15, 1889
It is a Quilt.
Miss Nettie Kelly, of Uniontown, has finished piecing a calico quilt of the saw tooth, or half square pattern containing 13,122 pieces, or 937 sq-rs. Each square is composed of 18 pieces of calico and muslin, about an inch square when the two half squares were joined. Can any fair damsels of Frederick beat that?

New Oxford Item
New Oxford, Pennsylvania
August 9, 1889
Mrs. Jas. Smith, of Mountpleasant township, recently presented a quilt to her nephew that contained 14,400 patches. The quilt contained 25 yds. of calico; two squares of the quilt contain 100 colors each and there are 324 colors in the entire quilt. The quilt was pieced and quilted by Mrs. Smith and is a wonderful and ingenious piece of handiwork.

Gettysburg Compiler
Gettysburg, Pennsylvania
August 13, 1889
A quilt presented by Mrs. Jas. Smith, of Mountpleasant township, to a nephew contains 14,000 patches.

Gettysburg Compiler
Gettysburg, Pennsylvania
January 14, 1890
              and
New Oxford Item
New Oxford, Pennsylvania
February 14, 1890
              and
The New Era
Humeston, Iowa
February 19, 1890
  After 47 years of assiduous labor Mrs. S. Lizzie Weaver, a Bridgeton, N. J. woman has just finished a crazy quilt of 30,075 patches.

New Oxford Item
New Oxford, Pennsylvania
February 21, 1890
  Rosa Stanhour, of Arendtsville, has completed a quilt composed of 12,168 patches; her sister Minnie has one of the same number nearly finished, and their sister Ida has made one of half that number.

The New Era
Humeston, Iowa
March 12, 1890
  Six Dubuque girls have just completed a bed quilt of 4,400 pieces, which will now be sold charitable purposes.

Cambridge Jeffersonian
Cambridge, Ohio
March 20, 1890
  Mr. and Mrs. Rev. G. E. McMana-

man were made the recipients of a large and beautiful silk quilt and pillow shams by the members of Ragan's Chapel church of which he has charge. The quilt contains 44 squares and 1300 pieces set together in a new and novel style. Each square was pieced by a different member of his church, and contains the name of the donor artistically worked in glowing silk colors. The quilt and shams are trimmed in rich ecrue lace and lined with cardinal selesia of a very superior quality. The quilt was presented to him on last Saturday and proved quite a surprise.

Fort Wayne Sentinel
Fort Wayne, Indiana
November 22, 1890
  Mrs. Wm. Weikert is making a quilt which as far as constructed contains over three thousand pieces, and when completed will contain about five thous-and pieces.

Woodland Daily Democrat
Woodland, California
January 26, 1891
  Miss Ella F. Kidd, of Keene, Ky., in 1885 completed a crazy quilt of 107,000 pieces, put together with 948,686 stitches!

New Oxford Item
New Oxford, Pennsylvania
February 27, 1891
  Miss Sallie R. Orner, of Menallen township, has just completed a patch-work quilt containing 1,694 patches.

HERRINGBONE, quilt top, c.1890, cotton, 78 x 84 inches, 720 pieces.
This quilt top is in the collection of Sue Reich, Washington Depot, Connecticut.

Chillicothe Constitution
Chillicothe, Missouri
March 6, 1891
  Mrs. John W. Goff, residing near
Blue Mound post office, has pieced a
quilt of 5,500 pieces, using six
spools of thread to do it. Come to
Livingston Co. for quilts.

Trenton Evening Times
Trenton, New Jersey
March 12, 1891
  Miss Mary Lindenberg, of Quakertown,
N. J., after two years' patient labor, has
completed a quilt 2 yards wide by 2 ¼ long,
which contains 23,228 distinct pieces.

Woodland Daily Democrat
Woodland, California
April 18, 1891
                    A Quilting Party
  A quilt composed of 5,600 blocks
was quilted by the guests of Mrs. W.
G. Hunt Friday, April 17th. The name
"A quilting party" brought every-
body out: why we would have gone
if it had rained pitchforks. Flowers
in purple, scarlet, and orange were
massed everywhere. The sun came
out and the day was quite perfect.
                              Guest.

Oshkosh Daily Northwestern
Oshkosh, Wisconsin
September 22, 1891
  Mrs. Sarah A. Jones, an
inmate of the Home for the Friend-
less, nearly eighty years old, exhibits
a patch work quilt made of 1,900
pieces.

The Standard
Ogden, Utah
May 19, 1892
   Mrs. William Davis, of Royalton, Pa.,
has a quilt which contains 10,800 silk
patches. Black and garnet seem to pre-
dominate. The design is original. She
also has a delaine quilt of a very pretty design, but not quite so many patches.

Edwardsville Intellegencer
Edwardsville, Illinois
July 13, 1892
   The young ladies of the Christian
Church at Centralia made a silk quilt
composed of over 1,000 pieces. There
are 800 names of persons embroidered
on the different pieces, each representing
10c for the benefit of the church. After
it was completed it was offered for sale,
to further swell the church fund, and
was purchased by a St. Louis lady for
$25. It is a remarkable piece of needle
work, and has netted the church over
$100.

Trenton Times
Trenton, New Jersey
November 9, 1892
        and
The Standard
Ogden, Utah
November 16, 1892
   Mrs. George W. Buell, of Meriden
Conn., has made a bed quilt which
contains 1,116 pieces of silk.

Denton Journal
Denton, Maryland
February 25, 1893
  A Frankford lady is making a quilt
which will contain 3,000 triangular
pieces.

Hopewell Herald
Hopewell, New Jersey
March 16, 1893
  Mrs. E. R. Honsley has just fin-
ished quilting a bed quilt consisting
of 3,905 pieces.

Gettysburg Compiler
Gettysburg, Pennsylvania
April 11, 1893
  Mrs. Jacob Heagy, of Butler township,
has pieced and quilted a quilt having 12,-
253 patches and about 254,496 stitches.
Mrs. Heagy did the work in the sixty-second
year of her age.

The Evening News
Lincoln, Nebraska
August 15, 1893
  Mrs. Mattie Wooten of Viola, Tenn., has
a quilt which is made up of 3,100 pieces. No
two of which are alike.

Gettysburg Compiler
Gettysburg, Pennsylvania
August 22, 1893
  Miss Mary A. Yeatts, daughter of Mr.
H. S. Yeatts, of near Heidlersburg, has com-
pleted a quilt containing 6,400 patches.

Weekly News
Frederick, Massachusetts
September 28, 1893
Made by Her Own Hands.
Mrs. Hart, of Carlisle Pa., has a fancy quilt which contains 7,752 pieces. Each one is but little over an inch square. She did all the work herself and justly feels proud of it.

Denton Journal
Denton, Maryland
February 10, 1894
Mrs. Emma B. Johnson, of Concord, has just finished a bed quilt with eleven hundred and ten pieces, no two alike. She calls it "Job's trouble."

Herald & Torch Light
Hagerstown, Maryland
May 3, 1894
A Quilt of Many Pieces.
Mrs. John Snavely, Sharpsburg, pieced a cradle quilt for her little granddaughter, May Ruth Lamm, that contains one thousand and three squares Mrs. Snavely is 78 years of age.

Herald & Torch Light
Hagerstown, Maryland
May 3, 1894
A CONTEST BETWEEN WOMEN.
Quite a rivalry has sprung up between the dames of Carroll county,

Md. and Adams county, Pa. as to which possess the elaborately pieced quilt. Mrs. Francis L. Criswell, of Carroll county is ahead up to date, with a quilt containing 10,930 pieces.

The Wellsboro Agitator
Wellsboro, Pennsylvania
August 1, 1894

AFFAIRS IN DELMAR.

Mrs. Amy Field, one of the oldest residents of this township, has since entering her 78th year pieced a quilt containing 1,008 pieces for her daughter, Mrs. John M. Butler, and one containing 752 pieces for her granddaughter, Mrs. James McKechney, of Blossburg. She is now piecing a quilt containing 1,008 pieces for her daughter-in-law, Mrs. Darwin Field, which she expects to finish before her 79th birthday—the 18th of August. The quilts are all made of silk, and they are very handsome. Mrs. Field is enjoying the best of health, and it has been years since she has seen a sick day.

Bangor Daily Whig and Courier
Bangor, Maine
November 7, 1894

Sagadahoc.

An inmate of the Old Ladies' Home at Bath is spending her days in sewing and counting, sewing and counting. She is making a crazy quilt and so far has put fourteen million, nine hundred and five thousand, six hundred and five stitches into it.

The Hopewell Herald
Hopewell, New Jersey
February 7, 1895
  Mabel Heath has been with us a
couple of weeks. While here this
time she finished piecing a bed-
quilt which she began about four
years ago. She has worked on it
in her vacations, when she has been
here. It contains eighteen hundred
and eighty-five blocks. It is on the
brick work pattern. She has pieced
just half of it since she has been
here this time.

Gettysburg Compiler
Gettysburg, Pennsylvania
February 26, 1895
  Mrs. W. H. Bower, of Huntington
township, has just completed a bed quilt
containing 12,100 separate and distinct
patches.

Gettysburg Compiler
Gettysburg, Pennsylvania
May 21, 1895
  Miss Osia Bittinger, of Menallen town-
ship, completed a quilt with 4,384
patches.

Olean Democrat
Olean, New York
June 14, 1895
  Mrs. Travis of Haskinville, Steuben
county, 80 years of age, has just com-
pleted a bed quilt on which she has been
working at odd times for three years.
It contains 3,276 pieces.

Marion Daily Star
Marion, Ohio
July 14, 1895
  Mrs. Mattie Wooten of Viola, Tenn., is
the proud owner of a quilt made of 3,168
pieces of calico.

Salem Daily News
Salem, Ohio
September 24, 1895
Presented the Quilt.
  A beautiful silk quilt of twenty-
seven hundred pieces, made by Mrs.
Rev. Crouse of Columbiana, aged
seventy-five years, was presented on
Saturday afternoon to the Woman's
Foreign Missionary Society of the
Methodist Episcopal church of Canton
district.

Gettysburg Compiler
Gettysburg, Pennsylvania
December 10, 1895
  Miss Mama Little, of this town, made
a quilt that contained 13,680 pieces.

Gettysburg Compiler
Gettysburg, Pennsylvania
March 31, 1896
  MRS. MARY DAUGHERTY, who resides
with her daughter, Mrs. Calvin Stouffer,
Jersey Shore, Pa., has just completed a
bed quilt which contains 6,500 patches.
Mrs. Daugherty is 72 years of age and ac-
complished this wonderful piece of work
without aid of eyeglasses.

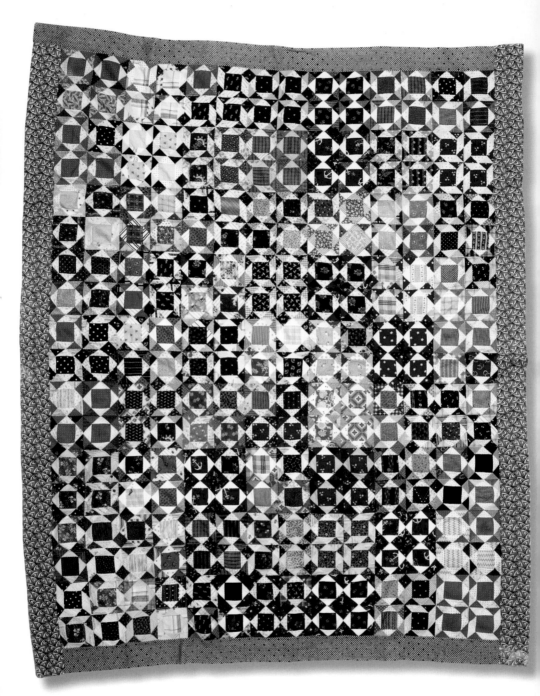

THE KING'S CROWN, variation, quilt top, c. 1900, cotton, 65 x 83 inches, 3,276 pieces. This quilt top is in the collection of Sue Reich, Washington Depot, Connecticut.

Gettysburg Compiler
Gettysburg, Pennsylvania
April 21, 1896
  Mrs. GEO. H. DUTTERA, of Mt. Tabor,
has finished a quilt containing 16,120
patches.

Indiana Democrat
Indiana, Pennsylvania
May 21, 1896
          and
Salem Daily News
Salem, Ohio
June 22, 1896
  Mrs. Mary Mahew of South Latrobe
has just completed a quilt of white and
red shades which contains 7,500 separate
pieces of cloth. Four large stars adorn
the outer edges, surrounded by a fancy
border. Five spools of thread were
used in quilting it and the owner has
refused a large sum of money for the
quilt.

Edwardsville Intelligencer
Edwardsville, Illinois
February 12, 1897
          The Billville Clarion
  Aunt Jane Poole has just completed
a quilt containing 2,649 pieces. The design is of her own get up, and it is a
dandy. Keep at it, Aunt Jane.

Bluefield Daily Telegraph
Bluefield, West Virginia
February 23, 1897
  Chicago.—The first public view was
given today of the quilt which is to be

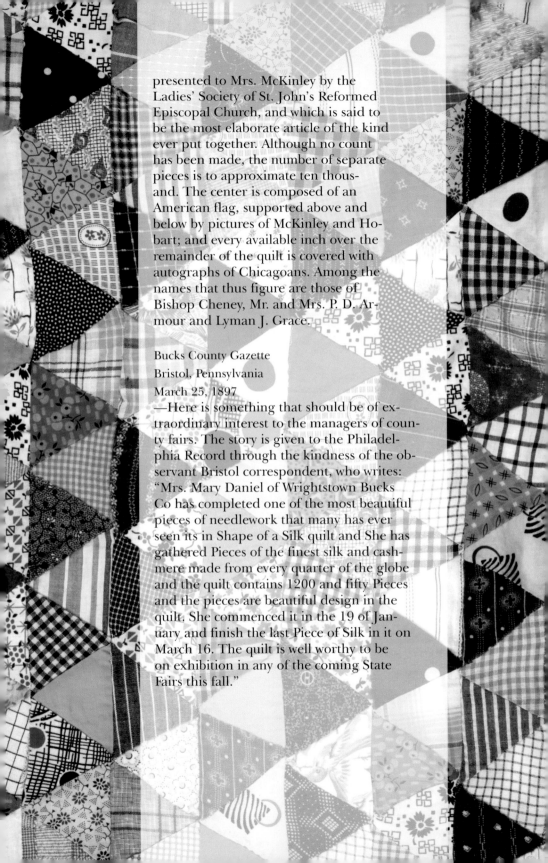

presented to Mrs. McKinley by the Ladies' Society of St. John's Reformed Episcopal Church, and which is said to be the most elaborate article of the kind ever put together. Although no count has been made, the number of separate pieces is to approximate ten thousand. The center is composed of an American flag, supported above and below by pictures of McKinley and Hobart; and every available inch over the remainder of the quilt is covered with autographs of Chicagoans. Among the names that thus figure are those of Bishop Cheney, Mr. and Mrs. P. D. Armour and Lyman J. Grace.

Bucks County Gazette
Bristol, Pennsylvania
March 25, 1897
—Here is something that should be of extraordinary interest to the managers of county fairs. The story is given to the Philadelphia Record through the kindness of the observant Bristol correspondent, who writes: "Mrs. Mary Daniel of Wrightstown Bucks Co has completed one of the most beautiful pieces of needlework that many has ever seen its in Shape of a Silk quilt and She has gathered Pieces of the finest silk and cashmere made from every quarter of the globe and the quilt contains 1200 and fifty Pieces and the pieces are beautiful design in the quilt. She commenced it in the 19 of January and finish the last Piece of Silk in it on March 16. The quilt is well worthy to be on exhibition in any of the coming State Fairs this fall."

Lima Times Democrat
Lima, Ohio
May 11, 1897
  A St. Albans (Vt) man has pieced a
bed quilt of 14,404 pieces.

Hornellsville Weekly Tribune
Hornellsville, New York
June 11, 1897
  Mrs. John Baily, of Cameron Mills,
has just completed a bed quilt of three
thousand, five hundred and twenty-
five pieces.

The Landmark
Statesville, North Carolina
September 17, 1897
  Wilkesboro Chronicle: Rev. W. L.
Dawson has a curiosity in the shape
of a quilt. The quilt has 6,340
pieces in it, and was made by Miss
Annie Dawson 77 years ago.

Gettysburg Compiler
Gettysburg, Pennsylvania
November 2, 1897
  Miss Lizzie Eyster made a quilt that
contains 3,024 patches.

The Landmark
Statesville, North Carolina
November 19, 1897
  Miss Sally B. Patterson has a quilt
which contains 10,300 pieces; in-
cluding the binding there are 10,301.
She made the quilt when a small
girl.   L.
Stony Point, N.C. Nov 16, 1897

The Landmark
Statesville, North Carolina
February 8, 1898
  Miss Daisy Lawson is the proud
owner of a quilt, presented to her by
Miss Narcissa Cavin, that has 2,446
pieces in it. This shows that we have
people who have a wonderful amount
of patience; especially so when we
consider Miss Cavin's age and health.

Hopewell Herald
Hopewell, New Jersey
March 23, 1898
—Mrs. Peter O. Voorhees has a bed
quilt that contains 5,600 blocks.

Naugatuck Daily News
Naugatuck, Connecticut
July 30, 1898
  Mrs. Philip Hubbarb of Palmyra,
Me., who claims to be the oldest lady
granger in Somerset county, has pieced
seven quilts since November, one of
them called the white house steps,
with 2,543 pieces in it, another with
1,225 squares, another silk quilt very
handsome, also a worsted crazy patchwork quilt, a very large one she has
made an outlined tidy worked in yellow silk, also a white, outlined spread
and pillow shams, a very nice piece
of work.

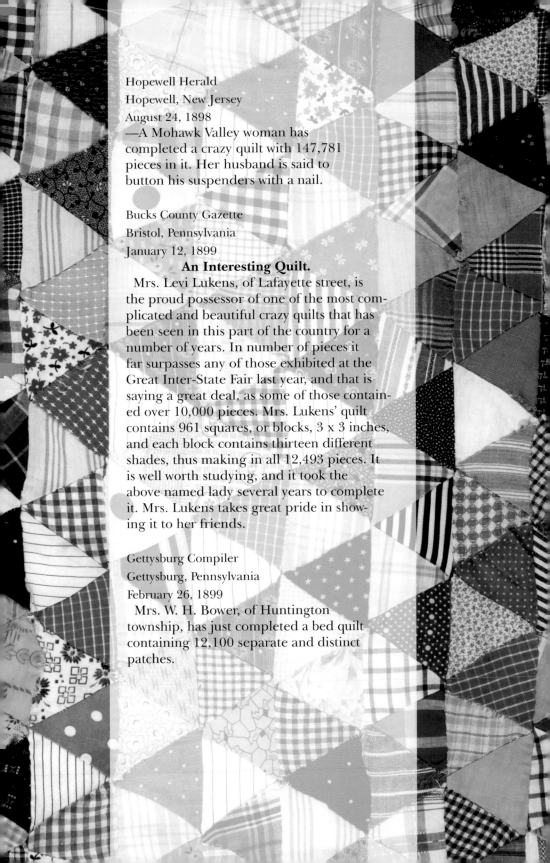

Hopewell Herald
Hopewell, New Jersey
August 24, 1898
—A Mohawk Valley woman has
completed a crazy quilt with 147,781
pieces in it. Her husband is said to
button his suspenders with a nail.

Bucks County Gazette
Bristol, Pennsylvania
January 12, 1899

An Interesting Quilt.

Mrs. Levi Lukens, of Lafayette street, is
the proud possessor of one of the most com-
plicated and beautiful crazy quilts that has
been seen in this part of the country for a
number of years. In number of pieces it
far surpasses any of those exhibited at the
Great Inter-State Fair last year, and that is
saying a great deal, as some of those contained over 10,000 pieces. Mrs. Lukens' quilt
contains 961 squares, or blocks, 3 x 3 inches,
and each block contains thirteen different
shades, thus making in all 12,493 pieces. It
is well worth studying, and it took the
above named lady several years to complete
it. Mrs. Lukens takes great pride in showing it to her friends.

Gettysburg Compiler
Gettysburg, Pennsylvania
February 26, 1899

Mrs. W. H. Bower, of Huntington
township, has just completed a bed quilt
containing 12,100 separate and distinct
patches.

Trenton Evening Times
Trenton, New Jersey
March 5, 1900
  Mrs. Mary Hineline, of Durham
this county, has completed a quilt
which contains 5,226 patches.

Daily Kennebec Journal
Augusta, Maine
December 31, 1900
  Not all the wonderful quilts are
made by smart women. Here is
Elijah Rowe of Springvale, who has
made a quilt of silk that has about
3000 pieces in it, each piece the size of
a silver ten cent piece.

The Wellsboro Agitator
Wellsboro, Pennsylvania
May 8, 1901
              Composing Pieces.
  Mrs. Meddergrass—He comes of a
literurry family. His ma put over
1,000 pieces in a crazy quilt oncet.—
Baltimore American.

Trenton Evening Times
Trenton, New Jersey
July 17, 1901
   Aged Lambertville Lady Has Made
     Eight in Three Years Count-
          ing 57,133 Pieces.
      IS HALE AND HEARTY AT 78
   For a Person of Her Age Her Quilting
   Record Stands at Head of List So
   Far First Quilt Contained 9,000

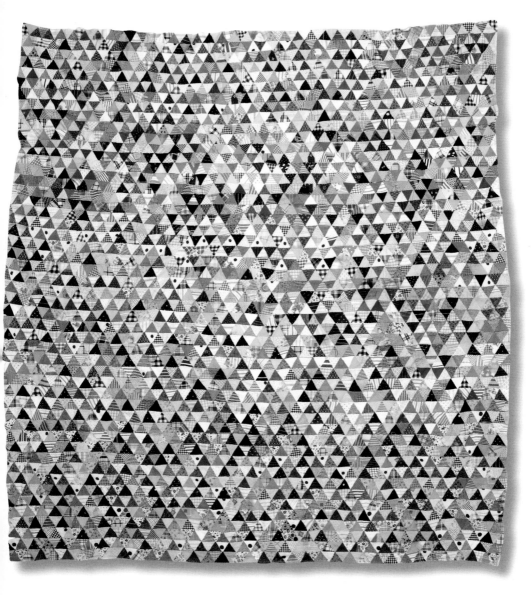

TRIANGLES, quilt top, c.1920, cotton, 66 x 84 inches, 3,550 pieces.
This quilt top is in the collection of Sue Reich, Washington Depot, Connecticut.

Pieces Most Famous One is Known As "Log Cabin Quilt."

Special to the Times.

Lambertville, July 17 – Mrs. Joel Allen, of South Main street, has a record for quilting that no doubt stands at the head of the list in the entire State, especially when it is taken into consideration that she is 78 years of age.

During the past three years she has completed, without assistance, eight quilts, that contain a total of 57,133 pieces. The first quilt contained 9,504 pieces; the second, 7,569; the third, 8,649; the fourth, 8,649; the fifth, 8,100; the sixth, 8,100; the seventh, called the "Log Cabin" quilt, 2,448, and the eighth contained 4,114 pieces.

CONTEMPLATES ANOTHER.

Mrs. Allen is still quite spry for a lady of her years, is good-natured and jovial, enjoys fair health and talks of commencing at an early day another quilt, which, if she lives to complete it, will be of a more fancy pattern than the others.

New Oxford Item
New Oxford, Pennsylvania
April 11, 1902

Novel Piece of Patchwork

John Billingsley, an inmate of the Soldier's Home, has completed a unique patchwork quilt upon which he has been working for two years past. The quilt is made entirely of satin and sateen, and is designed to depict the glories of the Union as they appear to an old soldier. There are 984 distinct pieces and 1,132,755

stitches in the article. The spread is a little over five feet square. In the centre is a large star, made up of small diamond-shaped pieces. In this star are set portraits of Washington, Lincoln, Grant, Garfield and McKinley, photographed upon silk. The star is surrounded by 24 badges of the army corps of the civil war and by 45 national flags, representing each state. Then there are the flags of eight foreign nations with which the United States at some time or other has been engaged in war.

The quilt is bordered with parallel stripes of red, white and blue and edged with fine gold fringe. The whole is artistically put together and reflects credit upon the workmanship of the maker.

Billingsley was a member of the Eighty-first Pennsylvania when the civil war began, but later entered the service of the regular army.—Washington Post.

Gettysburg Compiler
Gettysburg, Pennsylvania
April 22,1902
Mrs.John Howard,of Scotland, Franklin county, has just completed a quilt that contains 11,088 pieces. She had been working on that quilt for about three years.

New Oxford Item
New Oxford, Pennsylvania
October 3, 1902
Grandmother Miller, of Two Taverns, has completed a quilt which contains 2,-250 patches.

Bucks County Gazette
Bristol, Pennsylvania
February 12, 1903
  Mrs. Bertice Douglass has just comple-
ed a bed quilt which has ten thousand and
eighty pieces in it.

Altoona Mirror
Altoona, Pennsylvania
November 24, 1903
  Mrs. Elizabeth McIntyre, of Quarry-
ville, at the age of 81, has just completed a silk quilt containing 1,775
patches, log cabin pattern. The silk of
one patch is 114 years old.

Daily Kennebec Journal
Augusta, Maine
February 1, 1904
  Mrs. Mower is one of the sweetest and
best old ladies in New England, among
the happiest and liveliest of those who
reside in the State. Wonderfully pre-
served she gets about the house without the assistance of anyone. She is a
good writer and each Sunday sends a
good long letter to her daughter in
Minneapolis.
  During the year 1899 she made twelve
patchwork quilts, five of them having
1200 pieces. They included crazy quilts
log cabins, silk and various patterns.
Hundreds of stitches and yet the needle
work is perfection, and each piece daint-
ily fastened with fine and regular work.
"Yes," says she, "I should be miserable
if I did no work and I spend the greater part of my time in sewing. I had
rather do it than anything else."

BLAZING STAR, quilt top, c.1900, cotton, 89 x 98 inches, 900 pieces.
This quilt top is in the collection of Sue Reich, Washington Depot, Connecticut.

Daily Kennebec Journal
Augusta, Maine
May 11, 1904
  Mrs. A. C. Plummer, aged 77 years, has made, this winter, three quilts, one of which has 1525 pieces in it.

The Wellsboro Agitator
Wellsboro, Pennsylvania
May 24, 1905
—Mrs. Isaac F. Swan, of Morton, Delaware county, aged 75 years, has completed a quilt containing 2,400 silk patches and 2,000 flower designs. She began making the quilt three years ago.

Bucks County Gazette
Bristol, Pennsylvania
October 5, 1905
Aged Woman Wins Prize.
  Mrs. Benjamin Tomlinson, a well-known resident of this borough, was awarded first prize at the Inter-State Fair, Trenton, this season, for the exhibition of a cotton patchwork quilt which contained 9,961 pieces. Mrs. Tomlinson is 75 years of age and the piecing of the quilt represented days of painstaking skill and patience, and final triumph of wonderful quilting, that could be equalled by few and excelled by none of half her age.

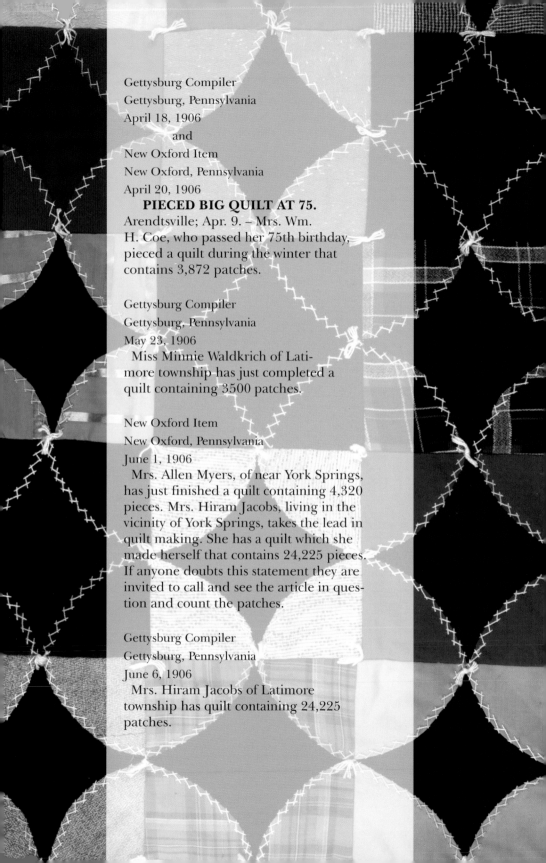

Gettysburg Compiler
Gettysburg, Pennsylvania
April 18, 1906
                and
New Oxford Item
New Oxford, Pennsylvania
April 20, 1906

PIECED BIG QUILT AT 75.
Arendtsville; Apr. 9. – Mrs. Wm.
H. Coe, who passed her 75th birthday,
pieced a quilt during the winter that
contains 3,872 patches.

Gettysburg Compiler
Gettysburg, Pennsylvania
May 23, 1906
  Miss Minnie Waldkrich of Lati-
more township has just completed a
quilt containing 3500 patches.

New Oxford Item
New Oxford, Pennsylvania
June 1, 1906
  Mrs. Allen Myers, of near York Springs,
has just finished a quilt containing 4,320
pieces. Mrs. Hiram Jacobs, living in the
vicinity of York Springs, takes the lead in
quilt making. She has a quilt which she
made herself that contains 24,225 pieces.
If anyone doubts this statement they are
invited to call and see the article in question and count the patches.

Gettysburg Compiler
Gettysburg, Pennsylvania
June 6, 1906
  Mrs. Hiram Jacobs of Latimore
township has quilt containing 24,225
patches.

New Oxford Item
New Oxford, Pennsylvania
December 27, 1906
Mrs. Elizabeth Smith, of Worman, the champion quilt maker of Berks county, finished 18 quilts in three years, each containing 1399 patches, making a total of 24,646 patches.

New Oxford Item
New Oxford, Pennsylvania
February 7, 1907
Mrs. Kate R. Albert, of near Gardner's Station, has just completed a quilt containing 11,664 patches, it being the second one finished in the past three years.

Denton Journal
Denton, Maryland
March 9, 1907
Mrs. Sarah Carmine, aged seventy years and blind in one eye, has pieced a bed quilt of an assortment of goods, containing twenty-six hundred blocks, having done the work in about twelve days.

The Perry Daily Chief
Perry, Iowa
June 25, 1908

HAS A
QUILT SHE
PRIZES HIGHLY

Mrs. A B Campbell has One Piece Made
By An Aunt Who is Totally
Blind

Mrs. A. B. Campbell received a few days ago, a quilt of which she is exceptionally proud. To the ordinary casual observer the quilt is not out of the ordinary run of fine bed quilts, but the circumstances which surround it makes it vulnerable.

The quilt contains one thousand five hundred pieces. It is black and white and was made by Mrs. Campbell's aunt. The aged lady is totally blind, yet she did all the work by herself. She used a self threading needle made especially for the blind yet she matched every piece and made not a single mistake in it all.

The work is finer than most quilts are that are made by people with a good eye sight. Mrs. Campbell's aunt lives at Griswold.

Bucks County Compiler
Gettysburg, Pennsylvania
October 4, 1908
Mrs. Edward Bruden got second prize on quilt work. In Mrs. Bruden's quilt were 1008 pieces which had been made since February of this year.

Gettysburg Compiler
Gettysburg, Pennsylvania
April 8, 1908
Mrs. J. A. Cline of Idaville has pieced a quilt that contains 3360 patches.

Gettysburg Compiler
Gettysburg, Pennsylvania
April 29, 1908
Mrs. Sarah Dahr, an aged lady of near York Springs, recently completed a quilt containing 5280 patches.

MALTESE CROSS, quilt, dated 1918, wool, 1125 pieces.
This quilt is in the collection of Sue Reich, Washington Depot, Connecticut.

The Wellsboro Agitator
Wellsboro, Pennsylvania
May 19, 1909

TIOGA COUNTY LOCALS

**Happenings of General Interest in
This County.**
—Miss Maud Jackson, of Ansonia,
has just completed a handsome bed-
quilt containing 2 900 pieces.

Edwardsville Intelligencer
Edwardsville, Illinois
November 27, 1909
  J. T. Mooney, 314 Hillsboro.
Fancy Quilt – On Saturday, tomorrow afternoon, a silk quilt of 3800
pieces will be raffled at 20 c. a number at the Palace store, also on the
following Wednesday afternoon; take
a chance. JULIET BARNETT.

Gettysburg Compiler
Gettysburg, Pennsylvania
March 17, 1909
  MRS. SAMUEL SPANGLER of Flat
Bush, Adams County, has just finish-
a quilt with 1920 patches.

Gettysburg Compiler
Gettysburg, Pennsylvania
February 2, 1910
  Mrs. George Strasbaugh of near
Berlin Junction has a quilt with 14,336
patches.

Adams County News
Gettysburg, Pennsylvania
February 19, 1910
  Fountain Dale, Feb. 18 – Mrs. Jennie
Gantz last week succeeded in quilting

a quilt which contains 72 blocks, each block having 10 pieces, a total of 1152 pieces.

Adams County News
Gettysburg, Pennsylvania
February 18, 1911
   Miss Rose Stahl has just completed a quilt containing 8319 patches.

Gettysburg Compiler
Gettysburg, Pennsylvania
February 22, 1911
   Mrs. Wm. H. Coe of Beechersville in her 80th year pieced a quilt during the winter with 5566 pieces.

Evening News
Ada, Oklahoma
July 18, 1911

GREATEST DAY IN
HISTORY OF ADA
Over 5,000 People In Attendance—Farm Product, Live Stock and Other Exhibits Were of the Very Best—Program For the Day Carried Out in Detail.
   Quilt – Mrs. Lillian Cole. (This quilt contains 9875 pieces; the next nearest had 8277 pieces and a third had 7020 pieces.)

Gettysburg Compiler
Gettysburg, Pennsylvania
September 9, 1911
                and
Adams County News
Gettysburg, Pennsylvania
September 9, 1911

Woman Finishes Quilt with Over
Fourteen Thousand Pieces.
   Mrs. Abraham Hershey, of route 5 Gettysburg, has competed one of the

most remarkable quilts which has been made in Adams County in recent years. The quilt contains no less than 14400 pieces.

Adams County News
Gettysburg, Pennsylvania
September 23, 1911
  William H. Cole, of Beechersville, a veteran of the Civil War, for pastime during last winter pieced a quilt that contains 6022 patches. He also showed your correspondent tomato vines 17 feet long, bearing nice large tomatoes.

Gettysburg Compiler
Gettysburg, Pennsylvania
September 27, 1911
  MRS. ABRAHAM HERSHEY, living on Chambersburg pike near Marsh Creek, has completed a quilt of 14,000 pieces.

Adams County News
Gettysburg, Pennsylvania
September 30, 1911
Pieced Quilts
  Mrs. John McGLaughlin, of Fairfield, has just finished a saw tooth quilt containing 4712 patches. Miss Mollie McGlaughlin has pieced two quilts one of 3416 patches and the other 4536.

Gettysburg Compiler
Gettysburg, Pennsylvania
October 25, 1911
  MRS. U. L. GLATFELTER of East Berlin exhibited a patch quilt of 4627 pieces at the York Fair which took first premium.

Adams County News
Gettysburg, Pennsylvania
January 27, 1912

MADE THREE QUILTS

Mrs. Dennis E. Rice, of Benders-
ville, has completed three quilts, two
of which are 2 yards, 8 inches square,
the one containing 1600 patches and
the other 3328. The third quilt is two
yards square and contains 1572 patches.

Gettysburg Compiler
Gettysburg, Pennsylvania
February 14, 1912

Grace, the 9 year old daughter of
Mr. and Mrs. J. R. Loungenecker of
Fairfield has just completed a quilt
containing 3487 separate patches.

Gettysburg Compiler
Gettysburg, Pennsylvania
April 10, 1912

MISS LIZZY RUFF of New Oxford has
a quilt pieced by her that contains 10,-
130 separate patches.

Gettysburg Compiler
Gettysburg, Pennsylvania
April 10, 1912

MRS. GEORGE STRASBAUGH, of near
New Oxford, has a patchwork quilt
she pieced when a girl, that contains
13,346 patches.

Gettysburg Compiler
Gettysburg, Pennsylvania
May 1, 1912

MISS ELLA DELAP of Idaville has
just finished a patchwork quilt containing 4,256 patches.

Fitchburg Daily Sentinel
Fitchburg, Massachusetts
October 19, 1912

Mrs. M. A. Horton of West Stonington, Me., who is 89 years old, has during the past year made nine rugs and four patchwork quilts. One quilt contains 4930 pieces.

Trenton Evening Times
Trenton, New Jersey
December 14, 1912

QUILT HAD 1,000 BLOCKS

BURLINGTON, Dec.11.—A hundred patchwork quilts formed part of the effects of the late Asa W. Scholey, a hermit, which were sold at auction yesterday. The quilts saved for generations by the Scholey family once wealthy and prominent socially, were found in the hermit's abode after his recent death at the county almshouse. One of the quilts had 1,000 blocks of patches.

Daily Commonwealth
Fond Du Lac, Wisconsin
December 17, 1912

CRIPPLE PIECES QUILTS IN ORDER TO MAKE A LIVELIHOOD.

Former Resident Does Exacting Work at Oshkosh on a Sewing Machine Though he is Denied the Use of His Limbs.

Oscar Lewis, a cripple residing on Ashland avenue, Oshkosh, has adopted a novel way of earning a livelihood. The Lewis boy is a victim of infantile paralysis, as a result of which he is a cripple from the waist down. He left

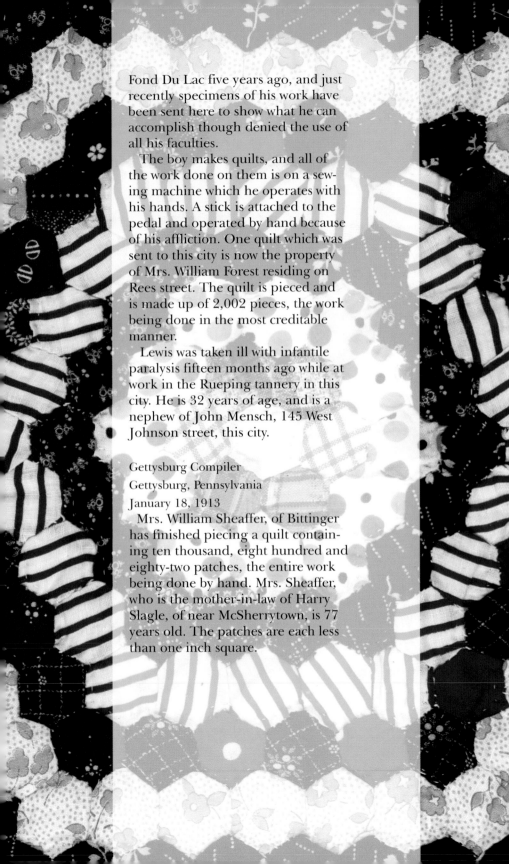

Fond Du Lac five years ago, and just recently specimens of his work have been sent here to show what he can accomplish though denied the use of all his faculties.

The boy makes quilts, and all of the work done on them is on a sewing machine which he operates with his hands. A stick is attached to the pedal and operated by hand because of his affliction. One quilt which was sent to this city is now the property of Mrs. William Forest residing on Rees street. The quilt is pieced and is made up of 2,002 pieces, the work being done in the most creditable manner.

Lewis was taken ill with infantile paralysis fifteen months ago while at work in the Rueping tannery in this city. He is 32 years of age, and is a nephew of John Mensch, 145 West Johnson street, this city.

Gettysburg Compiler
Gettysburg, Pennsylvania
January 18, 1913

Mrs. William Sheaffer, of Bittinger has finished piecing a quilt containing ten thousand, eight hundred and eighty-two patches, the entire work being done by hand. Mrs. Sheaffer, who is the mother-in-law of Harry Slagle, of near McSherrytown, is 77 years old. The patches are each less than one inch square.

Fort Wayne Sentinel
Fort Wayne, Indiana
February 4, 1913
GIVES PRESIDENT QUILT CONTAINING 5,982 PIECES.
Washington, Feb. 4. – President Taft's collection of gifts was increased today when he received a red, white and blue quilt from S. H. Read, of Merna, Neb., a civil war veteran, 82 years old, who wrote that the quilt had been made entirely by hand contained 5,982 pieces.

Adams County News
Gettysburg, Pennsylvania
March 8, 1913
Cashtown
Cashtown – Last week one day Mrs. G.W. Biesecker invited a few women to help her quilt a quilt that contained seventeen hundred and seventeen patches. This quilt was pieced long years ago by Mr. Biesecker's mother.

Evening Post
Frederick, Maryland
April 8, 1913
and
Trenton Evening Times
Trenton, New Jersey
November 19, 1913
Made 30 Quilts in 2 Years.
Miss Rebecca Ann Myers, residing near Chewsville, celebrated her eighty-second birthday by finishing the

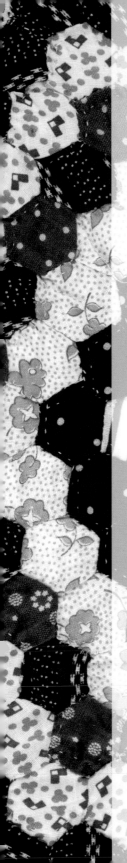

completed six bed comforts. For the past 32 years she has had a stand at the city market in Hagerstown and attends regularly every Saturday, rising at 2 and 3 a.m., and driving to Hagerstown with her produce.

Adams County News
Gettysburg, Pennsylvania
October 4, 1913

Letters of Interesting News From Adams County Towns

Mrs. T. J. Herman, residing along the State road at the edge of town is the owner of an "Irish Chain" quilt, made by Sophia Minter, and bears the date of 1853. She also has a quilt made by herself some years ago that contains 6241 pieces.

Lincoln Daily News
Lincoln, Nebraska
November 1, 1913

Guide Rock Signal: On the 26th of August, Mrs. Hannah Crow finished a fine quilt, which she had pieced since the first day of April, in which there were nine blocks of 346 pieces each, 3,114 pieces altogether. During this time she pieced also seven other quilts. The young women of this generation are not particularly interested in quilt work, but the older ones of the age of Mrs. Crow appreciate the work done in such a quilt.

Trenton Evening Times
Trenton, New Jersey
November 19, 1913

AT 89, SHE MAKES
CHRISTMAS GIFTS.

Mrs. Lydia Mount Taylor Has
Completed Novel Quilt of
512,000 Stitches.

Mrs. Lydia Mount of 930
Genesee Street is today one of the
happiest, most active and healthiest
old women in the city. She recently
celebrated the 89th anniversary of her
birth.

She arises every morning winter
and summer, at 5 o'clock and goes to
bed with the chickens. She reads
the Bible daily spends the most
of her time doing fancy sewing and
making fancy bed quilts. She takes
great pride in exhibiting, as a sample
of her skill in needlework, a won-
drously contrived patchwork bed quilt
that is the fruit of her own labor. It
is composed of 13,805 diagonal shaped
blocks, each one an inch square. The
blocks are pieces of calico accumu-
lated since she was a little girl and
in each block 40 stitches were taken,
thus making just 512,000 stitches that
Mrs. Taylor took. She had the quilt
on exhibition at both the Inter-State
and Mount Holly fairs.

Adams County News
Gettysburg, Pennsylvania
February 7, 1914

Mrs. George Fissel is quilting a
quilt for Mrs. Emanuel Bollinger that

had been pieced about 50 years ago
containing 5088 patches. The patches
are about an inch square and put together by overwhipping the seams
and each patch had a piece of paper
sewed in with the patch supposed to be
a pattern. If there is anybody that
can beat it in the State, we would be
glad to hear of them.

Gettysburg Compiler
Gettysburg, Pennsylvania
February 14, 1914
   MISS MAME COULSON, of Hunting-
ton township has completed a quilt
containing 2208 patches.

Adams County News
Gettysburg, Pennsylvania
April 11, 1914
              and
Gettysburg Compiler
Gettysburg, Pennsylvania
April 18, 1914
              Upper Huntington
   Upper Huntington – During the past
winter Miss Florence Miller pieced a
quilt containing 2324 patches.

Elyria Evening Telegram
Elyria, Ohio
May 19, 1914
              and
Wichita Weekly Times
Wichita Falls, Texas
May 22,1914
              Old Quiltmaker Is Dead.
   Colerain, O., May 19. — Mrs. Ruth
Hewling, 92, a Quaker woman famous

MOSAIC, quilt, c. 1920, cotton, 62 x 80 inches, 8,000 + pieces.
This quilt is in the collection of Sue Reich, Washington Depot, Connecticut.

for her quilts, is dead at her home
here. Mrs. Hewling is said to have
made fully 1,000 quilts and they are
scattered in many parts of the world.
For 12 years she was an invalid and
the 173 quilts she made in that time
were given to charity.

Adams County News
Gettysburg, Pennsylvania
March 4, 1916
  Mrs. Elizabeth Brenneman has
just completed a quilt containing
10,438 patches.

Lima Times Democrats
Lima, Ohio
March 22, 1916
MADE 2500 QUILTS;
DIES AT 92 YEARS.

  Washington., Ind. March 23.—
Mrs. Alice Bailey, 92, who said
to have pieced 3,544 quilts during
the past 50 years, is dead here at the
house of her daughter, Mrs. Robert
Schofield. Mrs. Schofield says her
mother, averaged one quilt each
week during the fifty years and that
they have been distributed among
her mother's friends in all parts of
the United States.
  Mrs. Bailey was born in Manchest-
er, England.

Mansfield News
Mansfield, Ohio
October 21, 1916
   Margrijane Kemble, assisted by
her mother, entertained six of her
grandmother's friends at dinner and
a quilting Friday, the quilt of over
4,000 patches having been pieced for
the child by her grandmother, Mrs.
Jane E. Bloor, 85 years young. A
very pleasant day was spent.

Middletown Times
Middletown, New York
November 2, 1917
County Fair at Presby-
terian Church
...Mrs. B. P. Flory exhibits a cover lid
made in 1840, which is a handsome
piece of work, and the knotted coun-
terpane displayed by Mrs. Lottie Nan-
ny is much spoken of. Mrs. C. W.
Arnold's display of a blue coverlid
is a gorgeous one, and because it is
200 years old it is highly treasured
by the owner. The total of 2,600
pieces are in the quilt exhibited by
Mrs. Josephine Clason.

Gettysburg Compiler
Gettysburg, Pennsylvania
April 12, 1919
   Mrs. Nell, of York Springs, recently
finished a quilt which contains 1655
patches.

Evening Telegram
Elyria, Ohio
May 29, 1919

**Grafton Red Cross
Made Splendid Showing.**

The Grafton Red Cross auxiliary has completed its quota and has closed the sewing rooms. Twenty-two quilts have been made by this society, and one was donated by Mrs. Wessell, 84 years of age. She made it by hand and it contained more than a thousand pieces. Mrs. Wilson made 18 quilt tops and Mrs. Reichard knitted 50 pairs of socks.

The Humeston New Era
Humeston, Iowa
May 19, 1920

Last Thursday at the W. H. Helt home the M. E. Ladies Aid finished a quilt the cover of which was pieced by Mr. Helt's sister, C. A. Helt, when she was eighty years of age; it contained 1,700 pieces.

Port Arthur News
Port Arthur, Texas
January 14, 1923

**Woman finishes Quilt
Bearing 10,000 Pieces.**

SALEM. Ind., Jan. 13,—Quilts generally are thought to belong to the days of many years ago, but seldom has a person done such work as has exhibited recently by Mrs. James B. Brown of this city. She completed a quilt, that is 72x90 inches and that contains more than 10,-000 tiny blocks, each block hexagonal

in shape. It is intricate in design
and the work is without flaw.

Mrs. Brown began her work many
months ago. The pattern for the
quilt is known as "Job's Troubles."

Indianapolis Star
Indianapolis, Indiana
January 21, 1923

2,115 – PIECE QUILT
FINISHED IN 25 YEARS

LaPorte, Ind., Jan. 20,—Mrs. John
Smith of Washington, Ind., has completed a quilt she has been working on
for twenty-five years and which contains 2,115 pieces.

Indianapolis Star
Indianapolis, Indiana
January 29, 1923

POSSESSES QUILT MADE UP
OF 7,224 HALF-INCH PIECES.

Richmond, Ind., Jan. 28. – A quilt
containing 7,224 pieces, which took her
ten years to complete, is owned by Mrs.
John K. Johnson, 404 North Eleventh
street, of this city. She has had it for
about forty-five years, she says. It
took first prize for three consecutive
years at the Union county fair. The
pieces are one-half inch square. Mrs.
Johnson said the interest which has
been aroused over home-made quilts in
Indiana recently has induced her to tell
the public about the one she owns.

Indianapolis Star
Indianapolis, Indiana
February 9, 1923

QUILT OF 22,178 PIECES.

Washington, Ind., Feb. 8 – Mrs.
Mary E. Fitzpatrick of Montgomery reports a quilt with a new record number
of pieces in it. Mrs. Fitzpatrick's quilt
contains 22,178 tiny pieces. It was made
years ago.

Decatur Review
Decatur, Illinois
April 17, 1923

BEAUTIFUL QUILT
TAKES MUCH WORK

*Estimate 25,000 Stitches Takes on 143
Blocks.*

A beautiful patchwork quilt is offered for sale in a local store for $50.
It was made by an Atlanta, Ill., woman who is quite old. It is frankly
admitted that it was doubted if it
will sell at this price. It is a wonderful example of handiwork and
every piece in it is of silk velvet. A
little calculation was made as to the
amount of labor involved in the making.

The quilt is composed of six inch
blocks and was eleven blocks wide
by thirteen blocks long, a total of 143
blocks. Each blocks is composed of
six strips each about an inch wide
by six inches long. There are 958 of
these silk velvet strips in the quilt.
It was sewed with a cross stitch,
twenty-six stitches to each strip.

25,000 STITCHES.

A little calculation shows that a total of 22,308 stitches were required in combining the strips into a quilt. This does not take into account the border or other extra work that was done. Allowing 2,692 for the number of extra stitches this brings the grand total up to 25,000 which is probably too low. At the rate of $50 for 25,000 stitches the maker of the quilt would receive two-tenths of a cent a stitch or one cent for five stitches.

An expert needle woman would be able to make fair wages at this rate. But the big item of cost of this quilt was not in the labor but in the material. It will be remembered that the pieces are all silk velvet. Some of them were odds and ends, no doubt but it is practically certain that much of it was bought new.

Then there are the thread and the lining and other trimmings which are no small item. The woman who made this quilt offers to make one just like it for $15 if she is furnished with all the material. At that price should make sixteen stitches for a cent, to say nothing of cutting, fitting and other work. Making quilts for the market would seem to be no get-rich-quick scheme.

Wisconsin Rapid Tribune
Wisconsin Rapids, Wisconsin
July 9, 1923

Mrs. Charles Chick, of Oskaloosa, Iowa, possesses a quilt containing 3,116 separate pieces.

The Deming Herald
Deming, New Mexico
August 31, 1923
An Indianapolis woman has pieced and quilted a quilt containing 30,308 red, white, and blue pieces. She values it at $1,000.

Zanesville Signal
Zanesville, Ohio
July 1, 1924
It is said of a Cleveland Man that has just finished making a patchwork quilt which contains 26,664 pieces and some how or other we imagine his name is Percy even if he is or was persistent.

New Oxford Item
New Oxford, Pennsylvania
February 19, 1925
Mrs. Wm. Huff, New Chester, has completed a quilt having 2500 patch-es.

Gettysburg Compiler
Gettysburg, Pennsylvania
March 14, 1925
Mrs. Elizabeth Brenneman and Hettie Boyer, of Mummasburg, have finished a quilt, in which there are 6304 patches.

The Frederick Post
Frederick, Maryland
April 27, 1926
The White House is being redeco-rated. The plan is to gradually fur-

nish all the rooms in antique, early American furniture. And many people possessing such treasures are donating them to this purpose. One of these gifts is a square patchwork quilt. It is composed of many small squares. But it is too small for any of the beds in use at the present time. The person in charge of the redecoration thinks he can utilize it by enlarging the square, one row each way. So he is having 177 more squares made.

These will be just exactly enough to increase the quilt to the desired size.

How many small squares are there in the quilt in its original form?

The Frederick Post
Frederick, Maryland
April 28, 1926

Last Puzzle Answer:
The square patchwork quilt, donated to the White House for use in redecorations, contains 7744 small squares. That is, it is an 88 x 88 square. If increased 1 row, it would be an 89 x 89 square and would contain 7921 small squares. This square is 177 squares larger than the original square quilt. (7744 + 177 = 7921). To solve a puzzle of this type divide the difference between the two squares by 2. The answer without the remainder (1-2) is the size of the smaller square.

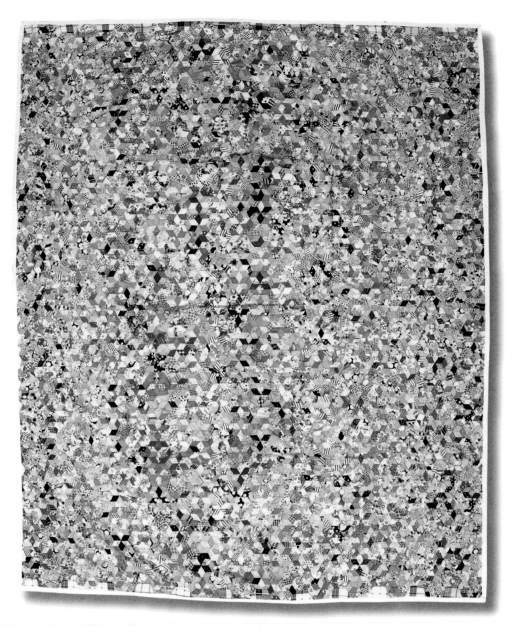

BABY BLOCKS, quilt, c.1925, cotton, 47 x 75 inches, 7,500 pieces.
This quilt is in the collection of Barbara Garrett, Pottstown, Pennsylvania.

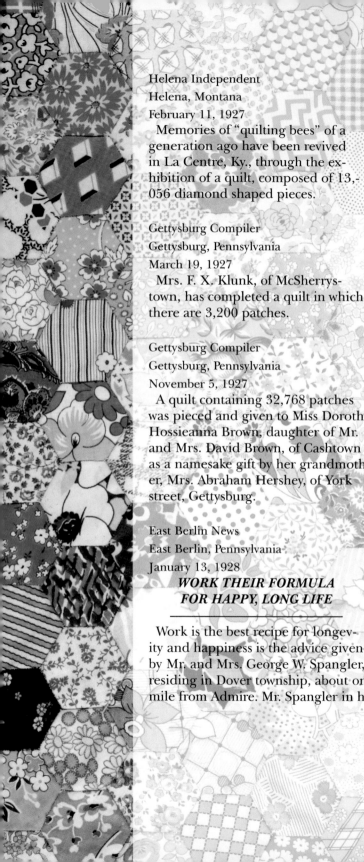

Helena Independent
Helena, Montana
February 11, 1927
  Memories of "quilting bees" of a
generation ago have been revived
in La Centre, Ky., through the exhibition of a quilt, composed of 13,-
056 diamond shaped pieces.

Gettysburg Compiler
Gettysburg, Pennsylvania
March 19, 1927
  Mrs. F. X. Klunk, of McSherrys-
town, has completed a quilt in which
there are 3,200 patches.

Gettysburg Compiler
Gettysburg, Pennsylvania
November 5, 1927
  A quilt containing 32,768 patches
was pieced and given to Miss Dorothy
Hossieanna Brown, daughter of Mr.
and Mrs. David Brown, of Cashtown
as a namesake gift by her grandmother, Mrs. Abraham Hershey, of York
street, Gettysburg.

East Berlin News
East Berlin, Pennsylvania
January 13, 1928
WORK THEIR FORMULA
FOR HAPPY, LONG LIFE

  Work is the best recipe for longev-
ity and happiness is the advice given
by Mr. and Mrs. George W. Spangler,
residing in Dover township, about one
mile from Admire. Mr. Spangler in his

83rd year and *Mrs. Spangler in her*
78th year, and they have been married
about 49 years, so they are well qual-
ified to advise those who would live
long lives in marital bliss.

Both Mrs. and Mr. Spangler enjoy
good health and are quite active. Mrs.
Spangler claims she is able to do her
work as at the age of 50. Being on
the job with her house work, making
rugs, comforts and quilts, is what
keeps her in good health, she says.
She has in her possession a quilt
which has 2,340 patches, and which
she made entirely herself. She is one
of the very few women still living,
in York county, who spun in her time,
and she delights in talking about it.
Mrs. Spangler is still a great believer
in the simple life.

"Early To Bed, Early To Rise"

The Spanglers believe in the adage
"Early to bed and early to rise, etc."
They retire early each evening at 7 o'clock
and get up in the morning at 4 or
4:30 o'clock. This schedule they fol-
low faithfully the whole year around.
They are of the opinion that the
present generation does not get
enough rest.

Both Mr. and Mrs. Spangler have
lived in York county all their lives.
Mr. Spangler spent most of his time
in the Spangler valley where he was
raised. Mrs. Spangler was before
her marriage Amanda Sunday, and
lived near Davidsburg. They have
two sons, one the proprietor of a
music store in Harrisburg, and the other
manager of a clothing store in
York.

Gastonia Daily Gazette
Gastonia, North Carolina
February 16, 1928
  A subscriber says: "Will J. F. B.
tell us the size of the pieces in a
quilt containing 4796 pieces?" Such a quilt can be seen at
Mr. J. R. Oates, Crowders Creek,
the work of Miss Ida.

Lima News
Lima, Ohio
March 12, 1931

OHIO WOMAN IS SEWING STORY OF LIFE IN QUILT.

7,500 Pieces of Different
Colors Tell Joys and Sor-
rows of 65 years.

  ST. CLAIRSVILLE, O., March
12—(AP)—The story of her life
Miss Sarah Thompson, 75, has
sewn on her "quilt of gener-
tions," which she has just completed after 65 years of labor.
  There are the bright red and
yellow and white patches in the
quilt. These represent the gay
days of Miss Thompson's youth,
when she was the belle of the
cotillion and waltz in the age of
hoop skirts, top hats and softly
strumming guitars. They stand
for the merry winters of coast-
ing and skating, and the happy
summers of horseback riding.
They indicate the era of the
"gay nineties," when she glided
here and there thru this quiet
little city on her bicycle.

Then come the browns and blacks and greens, middle age! Hours by the fireside with her books.

Finally there are the grays, which are the most recently added patches, placed with her skillful fingers when they were not too occupied with housework and other useful tasks.

7,500 PIECES USED

There are 7,500 different pieces in the quilt—750 for every year she has lived, and more than this for every day she has labored on the article.

Miss Thompson has another hobby besides her remarkable "quilt of a lifetime."

It is the raising of canary birds. It might almost be said that the quilt was assembled to music. For ever since youth, Miss Thompson has been fond of her feathered friends. There are many of them now in her cottage here. They flit and cry in joyful glee at their mistress' voice.

Charleroi Mail
Charleroi, Pennsylvania
July 12, 1932

Quilt Contest
At Berryman's
Will End Today

A contest which is quite unique and which has created much interest particularly among the women of the community has been under way at Berryman's store since July 5th. It

is a quilt contest and ninety-three different quilts have been submitted for judging.

One of the features of the contest is the fact that some of the quilts are more than 100 years old. The oldest one submitted was made in 1765 and others are nearly that old. There are, too, quilts that are made of thousands of pieces. One is composed of 7396 patches and there are others with over 5000, 4000 and 8000 patches.

There are as many varieties as there are quilts in the contest. Among them are sunbursts, wool patch, double Irish chains, wedding rings, sunflowers, cross stitch, gold patch, tulip, flower garden, pine tree, Star of Bethlehem, Grandmother's fan, and many others.

The quilts have been sent in from many towns in the valley including Belle Vernon, Allenport, Monessen, Speers, Charleroi, and one from Ford City.

The contest will close today and the quilts will be kept on exhibition in the windows of the Berryman store until Thursday. The winners will be announced tomorrow.

Soda Springs Sun
Soda Springs, Idaho
April 20, 1933

IDAHO QUILT GOING TO WORLD'S FAIR

St. George—A "Twin State" pattern quilt, entirely hand made from over 4000 pieces, will be entered in the World fair at Chicago this summer by Mrs. Harry Pearce of St. George.

Each of the small blocks is slightly more than one inch in diameter hexagonal shape and the stars are six-pointed. The quilt has 12 star blocks, each made from 171 pieces. The pattern blocks are joined by other pieced sections made from 61 pieces.

It required three months of almost steady sewing to make the quilt top, and two weeks to quilt the top.

Charleroi Mail
Charleroi, Pennsylvania
September 11, 1933

QUILT OF 7,282 PIECES MADE BY CIVIL WAR VET

San Diego, Cal., Sept. 11 – All the women folks in this vicinity are jealous of a 78-year-old Civil War veteran, O.T. Simmons. The women are probably right in their jealousy because Simmons has just completed making a quilt containing 7282 pieces.

The veteran started quilt making as a hobby two years ago when he heard that a San Diego woman had won prize at the county fair for making a 6,000-piece quilt, he decided to beat her record. His 7282-piece effort was the result.

Reno Evening Gazette
Reno, Nevado
November 14, 1933

More than one thousand pieces of different material were used in a quilt just completed by Miss M. Thornton, aged seventy-six year, of Chadlington, England.

Reno Evening Gazette
Reno, Canada
December 13, 1933

Still Makes Quilt

Lake Park, Ia.,—(AP)—Christina Fenzel learned at the age of fifteen to piece quilts. Now, at the age of ninety-three, she estimates she has made more than one thousand quilts and is still busy at it. Last year she made twenty-three quilt tops.

Charleston Daily Mail
Charlestown, West Virginia
January 4, 1934

Mrs. C. A. Carpenter has spent 25 years collecting 1320 quilt patterns. Mrs. Dorothy Gaffey, of Chicago, has made a quilt from the autographs of famous women.

Charleston Daily Mail
Charlestown, West Virginia
April 14, 1934

USE 71,280 PIECES IN 100-YEAR OLD QUILT

LANCASTER, Pa.,—A hundred-year-old quilt made from 71,280 pieces of material is in the possession of Mrs. Richard Van Riper.

Very little is known about the history of the quilt, except that it was made about 1834 by Elizabeth Zell, who lived in Little Britain Township. near here.

By inheritance, the quilt went into the hands of Mrs. Arthur Bickham, who provided that her sister-in-law, the present owner, should have it upon her death.

It has been estimated that the work on the quilt required at least 10 years. There is some dispute as to whether most of the material used is old chintz, or oil chalice. The pattern is made up of 7,920 diamonds, each with nine tiny rosettes. Each rosette is made of a tiny circle of cloth, apparently cut around a dime. Half the diamonds have eight rosettes, with a red one in the center. This color scheme is reversed in the remaining half of the diamonds. Seen from different angles, the quilt shows hundreds of geometric designs of larger diamonds, pyramids and cubes. Held to the light, the quilt looks like old lace.

The quilt is 7 feet 11 inches long by 7 feet 2 inches wide. So fine is the needlework that the stitches scarcely can be seen with the naked eye.

Charlestown Daily Mail
Charlestown, West Virginia
April 27, 1934

QUILT CONTAINED 8,011 BLOCKS

REEDSPORT, Ore.,—A quilt containing 8,011 blocks, each containing three stitches, has just been completed by Uulla Paine. Centers of the block are gold, each surrounded by a different pastel shade. The third row is white.

A close-up of the unfinished back of this quilt shows the same style of mosaic paper-piecing used to construct the first quilt shown at the beginning of this book, made over one hundred years earlier. Paper piecing is a quilt construction technique still used by today's quiltmakers.

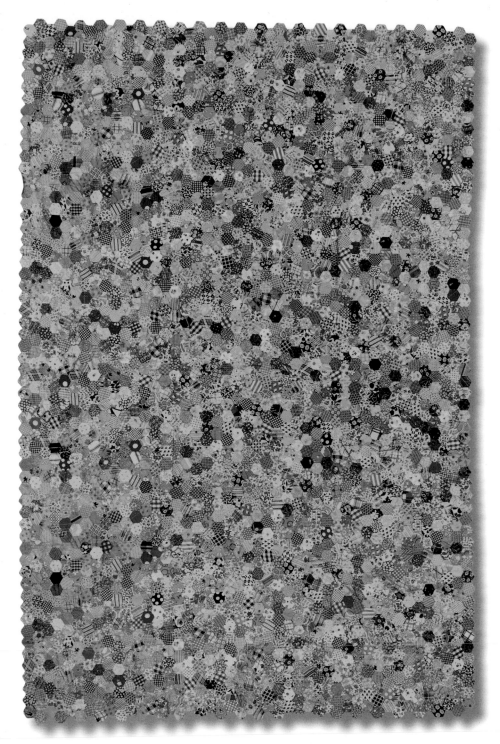

MOSAIC top, c. 1925, cotton, 60 x 89 inches, 2,677 pieces.
This quilt is in the collection of Barbara Garrett, Pottstown, Pennsylvania.